THE BOOK OF
THE PUG

by JOAN McDONALD BREARLEY

Frontispiece: The English import, Ch. Roualeyn Shere Khan, one of the stud forces at Shirley Thomas' Shirrayne Kennels in Flushing, New York.

Front cover: Ch. Nazrep Chingachgook, bred and owned by Lucille Perzan. Photo by D. Perzan.

Back cover: Waterside Royal Wind Song, C.D. owned by Susan B. Burnham, Waterside Pugs. Photo by Pet Portraits (Stankus).

ISBN: 0-87666-683-7

t.f.h.

Distributed in the U.S. by T.F.H. Publications, Inc., 211 West Sylvania Avenue, PO Box 427, Neptune, NJ 07753; in England by T.F.H. (Gt. Britain) Ltd., 13 Nutley Lane, Reigate, Surrey; in Canada to the book store and library trade by Beaverbooks Ltd., 150 Lesmill Road, Don Mills, Ontario M38 2T5, Canada; in Canada to the pet trade by Rolf C. Hagen Ltd., 3225 Sartelon Street, Montreal 382, Quebec; in Southeast Asia by Y.W. Ong, 9 Lorong 36 Geylang, Singapore 14; in Australia and the South Pacific by Pet Imports Pty. Ltd., P.O. Box 149, Brookvale 2100, N.S.W. Australia; in South Africa by Valid Agencies, P.O. Box 51901, Randburg 2125 South Africa. Published by T.F.H. Publications, Inc., Ltd, the British Crown Colony of Hong Kong.

Table of Contents

Acknowledgments

I wish to thank the many people who so willingly shared photographs of their dogs so that they could be recognized in this book dedicated to our wonderful breed.

A special thank you goes to Helen Bortner, who came up with so many valuable photographs from her own personal collection, as well as those of others, which include some rare old photographs of the dogs of yesteryear.

Alyce Andre and Shirley Kalstone graciously offered charming insights into the past history of our breed which have enhanced the book, and I am most grateful for their contribution. Thanks are due to Dr. Robert Shomer for veterinary counsel, to Stephen and Lillian McDonald for additional research, and to Sal Micelli for the candid About the Author photo.

Most of all I wish to express my sincere appreciation to Shirley Thomas who first suggested I write the book, and who was of immeasurable help in gathering material, both new and old. She always encouraged and offered information pertinent to the true portrayal of our breed.

Joan McDonald Brearley
New York City, 1980

Dedication

This book is for

SHIRRAYNE'S HONG KONG JADE EAST

my first and adored Pug bitch
and for her breeder

SHIRLEY THOMAS

Whose dedication and contribution to the breed
is inspirational and cannot be denied.

History

The Pug is of Chinese origin, dating back to about 400 B.C. However, as early as 600 B.C. "short-mouthed" breeds were mentioned in writings. Owned by the emperors of China, the Pug was held in high esteem and protected by palace guards. They even had their own servants to tend to their needs and desires. Thus were not only by royalty, but were among the favored pets of the Buddhist monasteries in Tibet.

Even today, Pugs were referred to as Lo-Chiang-sze, because it was said the __ __ first seen in the Chinese city of Lo-Chiang. They were also referred to __ __ Foo dogs, or foun dogs, because of the Himalayan legend that revealed a belief that if a man tended a prayer cage night after night it would turn into a Pug.

In ancient China a desirable characteristic of the Pug was the wrinkling on their foreheads. It was called a "prince mark" because its vertical lines formed by the wrinkles was __ __ resemble the ancient Chinese character for "prince." The elasticity of their skin was considered a most important feature.

A picture in an __ __ table, found in 1688, titled the Pug in line and color, __ __ lines existed in the Holy Land. The __ __ __ a painting where Christ __ __ dog resembling a Pug being at his feet.

THE PUG IN HOLLAND

The Pug was brought to Holland approximately 350 years ago by the crew members of the Dutch East India Trading Company. They called the breed the Chinese Mastiff. Because of the resemblance, it was believed the Pug had been bred down from the great Mastiff found in China. When the Pug reached England it was called the Dutch Mastiff, later called the Dutch Pug, and finally is Pug dog.

The Pug became popular in Holland almost immediately upon its arrival, and it was "the vogue" for women to promenade with

Chapter 1
History

The Pug is of Chinese origin, dating back to about 400 B.C. However, as early as 660 B.C. "short-mouthed" breeds were mentioned in writings. Owned by the emperors of China, the Pug was held in high esteem and protected by palace guards. They even had their own servants to tend to their needs and desires. Pugs were beloved not only by royalty, but were among the favored pets in the Buddhist monasteries in Tibet.

These ancient Pugs were referred to as Lo-Chiang-sze, because it was said they were first seen in the Chinese city of Lo-Chiang. They were also referred to as Foo dogs, or hand dogs, because of the Himalayan legend that revealed a belief that if a man handled a young eagle right after it hatched it would turn into a Pug. . . .

In ancient China a desirable characteristic of the Pug was the wrinkling on their foreheads. It was called a "prince mark" because the vertical "bar" formed by the wrinkles was said to resemble the written Chinese character for "prince." The elasticity of their skin was considered a most important feature.

A picture in an old Bible, found in 1958, dates the Pug to the time and place where Christ dwelled in the Holy Land. The picture is said to show a stoning where Christ has a dog resembling a Pug lying at his feet.

THE PUG IN HOLLAND

The Pug was brought to Holland approximately 350 years ago by the crew members of the Dutch East Indies Trading Company. They called the breed the Chinese Mastiff. Because of the resemblance, it was believed the Pug had been bred down from the great Mastiffs found in China. When the Pug reached England it was called the Dutch Mastiff, later called the Dutch Pug and finally Pug dog.

The Pug became popular in Holland almost immediately upon its arrival, and it was "the vogue" for women to promenade with

Young Dutch Champion Pematel's Aafje, a winner in Holland in 1974 who was bred and owned by Mrs. E. Tel. The sire was Warnsborn Symen ex Ch. Elsje von Bundeshaus. Photographed at 18 months of age by C. A. Veldhuis, Arnhem, Netherlands.

one of their "monkey-faced" Chinese dogs. They were also known as round headers, black-faced monk dogs, and were included as one of the "comforter" dogs, the small lap dogs used to keep their mistresses warm in the large unheated houses.

The Pug was not just a lap dog, however. William the Silent, King of Holland, was fond of Pugs and took his along with him when he waged war against the Spanish. A sound sleeper, he was awakened one night by the insistent barking, scratching and jumping of one of his dogs. He awoke just in time to avoid two would-be assassins that had slipped into his tent during the 1572 battle at Hermigny. As a result of this act of heroism, the Pug dog became the official dog of the House of Orange during the 16th century.

William Prince of Orange, great grandson of William the Silent, also adored Pugs. He took some of his Pugs with him when he crossed the English Channel and landed at Torbey in November, 1688 to ascend the throne of England. The Pugs were bedecked with orange ribbons attached to their collars to denote the family connection with the House of Orange. When his wife, Mary II, followed him in February of the following year, Pugs once again saw a surge in popularity, almost replacing the Maltese and King Charles Spaniels as court favorites. Pugs remained popular until 1866 when the Pekingese took over as number one.

THE PUG IN OTHER LANDS

There are reports bearing out the presence of Pugs in Russian court life in Moscow as early as the 16th century. It is said that they were also sold in the market place for the equivalent of ten cents. Some people theorize that the Pug may have reached Holland by way of Russia through Germany.

In Germany the Pug is called the Mopshond, as it is now called

William III, the Prince of Orange, who was a great admirer of the Pug breed. William journeyed with his Pugs when he crossed the English Channel to take the throne in England, and, befitting their association with the House of Orange, the Pugs wore orange-colored ribbons on their collars.

in Holland. It became popular in Saxony at the beginning of the eighteenth century and has become immortalized as the subject of countless pieces of treasured Meissen porcelains, which are highly prized and very expensive as collector's items.

The Pug, or *doguillo*, was present in Spain during the eighteenth century. This is borne out by the Goya painting of the Marquesa de Pontejos, rendered in 1785, which features a little Pug standing in the lower corner of the work of art.

By 1790 the breed had spread to France. Napoleon's Josephine had a Pug named Fortune that carried her messages back to Napoleon under its collar while she was imprisoned at Les Carmes. He is also said to have bitten Napoleon on their wedding night! Prince Lucien Bonaparte also owned Pugs.

The Pug was popular in Italy during the eighteenth century

Canadian Ch. First Young Lord and a chairful of his "kids." Bred and owned by Mr. and Mrs. Bernard Limoges, Ontario, Canada.

Future Dutch Champion Warnsborn Dieuwert je, photographed at six weeks of age. Bred and owned by Miss C.A. Veldhuis, the Netherlands. Sire was Duplex of Doms ex Warnsborn Aukje.

where the social set carted them around in their carriages and dressed them in fancy collars. Many pugs wore colorful little jackets with matching pantaloons. The Pug was called a *Cagnuolo* in Italy.

During all this time Pugs were seen in great numbers in Scotland and Ireland. They had fanned out from Northern England, the center of the Pug world, as word of their charm spread through all the neighboring countries.

THE ENGLISH STUD BOOK

The English stud book contains Pugs from as far back as 1859. The first volume of the Kennel Club Stud Book listed 66 Pugs. The first outstanding stud, however, was an apricot dog named Click (Lamb *ex* Moss), registered in 1875. He was the property of a Mrs. St. John. The book lists the sire, Lamb, as being a longhair from Peking. Both Lamb and Moss were said to have been captured in the Emperor of China's palace during the siege of Peking in 1860.

TWO EARLY BLOODLINES

The Pug reached one of its peaks of popularity during the reign of George III and Queen Charlotte of Mecklenberg. Mr. C. Morrison of Walham Green obtained a Pug of German origin for the Queen, who loved Pugs. Mr. Morrison bred apricot-colored Pugs and his first well known specimens were named Punch and Tetty. His line was highly thought of. The other early bloodline during this period was a line of silver fawns bred by Lord and Lady Willoughby de Eresby of Greenthorpe. Their stock was founded on a dog obtained in Vienna which was bred to a bitch brought from Holland in 1846. From these two Pugs a line of cold-stone fawns was established, peculiar because of their entirely black heads and large saddlemarks.

Two Pugs named Mops and Nell started the de Eresby line, but were eventually bred into the Morrison line and the interbreeding meant that a true line of neither descended.

Two other famous strains came along and were known as the Cloudy and Tragedy lines. The dog Lamb was the founder behind these. Mr. Fletcher, a prominent dog seller of the day, claimed, "They were plump and pretty and always wanted." He professed to selling between three and four hundred Pugs a year. This was also the period during which the early famous names in the breed began to appear: Mrs. Tulk's "long-haired" dog named Podkin, Mrs. Foster's Bradford Marvel (whose stud fee was a record one guinea), and Mr. Summer's famous Chotee, which he sold to Miss M. Garrod Keen for three hundred pounds!

During the reign of Queen Victoria the Pug received additional acclaim. While Victoria loved all animals, toy dogs were her particular penchant and she owned several Pomeranians, Pekingese and Pugs. Olga, Pedro, Minka, Fatima and Venus were the Pugs with which she started her breeding program. Bosco, one of her very favorites, was buried in Frogmore House Gardens in 1892. The grave is marked and the memorial still stands there today. It is acknowledged that it was largely on her interest in the dog fancy that the Kennel Club was formed in England in 1871. The Pug Dog Club was founded in England by Mr. T. Proctor in January, 1883. Later Pug clubs included the London and the Provincial Pug Dog Club, the Northern Pug Dog Club and the Scottish Pug Dog Club, which was founded in 1925.

Kaffir, featured on a post card dated June 1907, and owned by Lily Burden, England. Photo courtesy Shirley Thomas.

Harloo Ted's Boy, an Australian Champion owned by W. Gray of New South Wales, Australia. Ted's Boy was bred by Harry and Lou Green, Harloo Kennels, Shropshire, England.

THE FIRST DOG SHOW

The first formal dog show was held in 1859 for sporting dogs. While the Pug was admittedly no hunting dog, it was allowed to enter and compete. Nevertheless, none did! In 1860, however, there was a class for Pugs at the second Birmingham show.

THE BLACK PUG COMES ON THE SCENE

It is believed that the black Pug was developed in Japan around 900 A.D. During the ninth century they were supposedly brought into Japan as a result of a command from the Emperor in 824 demanding the Chinese government pay tribute to him by giving him two pai dogs. Pai was the name which was given to all short-legged dogs with small heads. The very first Japanese Pugs were black and white, or all black or all white, which some say accounts for the white on the chests of so many of the early black Pugs.

Hogarth's 1730 oil painting, *The House of Cards,* attests to the presence of the black Pug in Holland. Queen Victoria's black Pug was written about in the 1896 *Ladies Kennel Journal.* This dog was said to be an import from China and had a lot of white in its coat.

The first black Pug was shown at the first Pug Dog Club show in June, 1885. Lady Brassey exhibited a black Pug named Jack Spratt at the Maidenstone Show in 1886. It is believed by many that some of the early black Pugs owned by Lady Brassey were actually short-coated Pekingese which she purchased in China during her famed tour of the world aboard her yacht, *The Sunbeam*, in

Photographed on March 15, 1891 was Haughty Madge, one of the very earliest Pug dogs. Notice the lock on her collar, as well as the bow. Photograph courtesy of Helen M. Bortner.

1877. She mentions Pugs in her *A Voyage in the Sunbeam,* published in 1878.

It has always been a matter of discussion as to whether the Pug and the Pekingese were "one and the same" during those early years. Many hold that the Peke is actually a result of a breeding of the Tibetan Spaniel and the Chinese Pug. Whether those early dogs were short-coated Pekingese or long-coated Pugs is a moot question, especially when one recalls all the references to Click and Lamb and Podkin as being long-coated Pugs!

There was also a "rough-coated" Chinese Pug shown in England in 1884 by John Strugnell. This dog had his own business card which read, "Ratcatcher to Her Majesty Queen Victoria"—and he truly did rid her palace of rodents. He was named Strugnell's King Dick and was responsible for some of the early winning short-coated Pekingese of the time.

English Ch. Bo-Filbert of Ide, Best of Breed at the 1972 Chester Championship Show, was bred by Mr. J. H. J. Braddon. The owners are Mr. and Mrs. T. W. Hilder of Yorkshire, England. Diane Pearce photograph.

The first black Pug to really come anywhere near up to the Standard was Ch. Duke Beira, owned by Miss A.C. Jenkinson. Another was Ch. Chotee, purchased for two hundred pounds by a Mrs. Summers. This was said to be an excellent price, exceeded only by the purchase of Jack Valentine from his breeder Miss Neish by the Marquis of Anglesey for two hundred fifty pounds. Chotee was later sold for three hundred pounds to Miss M. Garrod Keen.

Other early breeders of the black Pugs in England were Mrs. Raleigh Grey, whose bitch Rodah was one of the best of its time, Mrs. Recketts, Mr. Kingdon, Miss H.C. Couper (later Mrs. Lake), Mrs. F. Howell and her Ch. Mister Dandy, and Dr. Tulk and his Ch. Bobbie Burns were famous in their time.

While the early black Pugs gained recognition, they never were to be as popular as the fawns, and part of the reason was said to be that they never carried the heavy wrinkling which distinguished the breed. It was not until 1897 that the Kennel Club opened separate color classes for blacks. It has only been since 1919 that really good quality blacks have been bred.

There were a few exceptions, however, that maintained the interest in the breeding of the blacks. Miss May Woolrich bought Ch. Lord Dalmeny, a black son of Bobbie Burns from her own famous black, Ch. Prince Pipkin, out of Hulcote Merry Girl. Miss Woolrich bred some high quality black Pugs. An eye injury cut short Lord Dalmeny's show career, but not before he won 22 Challenge Certificates and added to the preservation of this color.

Miss Rosa Little turned down five hundred pounds·for her black, Lady Mimosa, two months before she died! Lady Mimosa was said to be one of the most perfect bitches ever bred in England, a winner of five C.C.'s and 35 prizes before her early demise. At 8 months of age at her first show she won all the classes from Puppy Class on up to Open and got the C.C. for Best Black Bitch as well.

Ch. Young Scotland was a black bred by Mrs. Prowett Ferdinand. He was grandsire of The Laird of Otter, one of the pillars in the breed—either color! Mrs. Ferdinand's Ch. Rapture of Boscobel was winner of 16 Challenge Certificates and a prominent stud.

PUGS IN ENGLAND IN THE 20TH CENTURY

In the early decades of the twentieth century several prominent dog fanciers came along to promote the breed. Mrs. Hampden-Shaw's Turret Kennels were famous, as were Miss Rosa Little and her Valkyrie Kennels, Mrs. Benson and Mrs. Warden Gowring, to name a few. In 1914 Miss Woolridge, whom we mentioned earlier for her outstanding blacks, brought more than a half dozen dogs to a show and won all her classes! However, World War I put an end to her plans for her kennel. She did manage to finish her Ch. Towcester Touchwood after the war, which indicates her continued interest in the breed. Her Pug named Old Moore became an American champion; as did her Little Fly-A-Way, after they were exported to America.

Other prominent breeders and their dogs were Miss Spurling and her Ch. Princess Pretty (1920); Miss C. Smart and Ch. Captain Nobbs, winner of four C.C.'s; Miss M.D. Hatrick and Ch. Penella of Inver (1927); Mrs. Demaine's Ch. Dark Ducas; Miss Blanche Thompson and Ch. Fairlea Antonia; Mrs. M.C.G. Gibbon and her Ch. Dark Drummer; Mrs. C.C. Meese and Ch. Roy of Ellerslie; Mrs. Micklem's Golly Eyes of Bitchet; and Mrs. E.M. Power and her Broadway Pugs.

THE SECOND HALF OF THE 20TH CENTURY

While it would be impossible to name every Pug fancier who has contributed to the popularity of the Pug and its important bloodlines down through the years, there are several very active breeders that are helping to perpetuate the Pug through their breeding programs and exhibiting in the show rings. The Pug Dog Club, still active today, claims many devoted members.

In the 1960's the Martlesham Pugs were well known. Mrs. N. Gifford's Ch. Stormie of Martlesham had won 8 Challenge Certificates and was a stud force at her kennels and the sire of champions bearing the Martlesham suffix. Mrs. Brenda Banbury of Surrey is another breeder who uses the Flocktons suffix on her prize-winning Pugs. Mrs. A. Williams is another breeder whose Hoonme Kennel name is well-known. Her Ch. Paramin Polanaise of Hoonme was the 1975 Crufts Best of Breed winner.

Other current breeders, in alphabetical order, are: Mrs. E.S.

Shown taking a rest is Shirrayne's Le Petit Caporal Napoleon, owned by Mr. and Mrs. Paul G. Saurwein of New York City. Napoleon's sire was Shirrayne's Golddigger, ex Fabulous Fifi. Photo by Giovanni Rabadi.

Brown, Mr. and Mrs. W. Burrows, Mrs. J.P. Clark, Mrs. H.M. Enders, Mrs. P.J. Galvin and her Pegal Pugs, Mr. and Mrs. R. Gibson and their Elmsleigh Pugs, Mrs. M.E. Inge, Mrs. D. LeGallais and her Gais Pugs, Mr. M. Quinney and his famous champion Adoram Pugs, Mrs. P.S.H. Spencer Beighton and her Pyebeta Pugs, Mrs. N.E. Tarbitt's Nanchyl Pugs, Mrs. E.J. Thorp, Mrs. Susan Welch and her Skehana Pugs, Mrs. A.L. Weller and Mrs. W.S. Young and her Ryden Pugs.

The "success story" in the breed in Britain for the 1970's is the tale of Ch. Dingleberry Vega, top Pug in Britain for 1974, 1975 and 1976. Owned by Miss Lynda Appleton, Vega seems to have presented a considerable problem to her as a puppy. It seems he couldn't be housebroken, and was almost returned to his breeder on several occasions! With several Groups and twice Reserve Best at the championship shows, his patient owner now seems to have been rewarded for her trouble!

HARLOO

Two of the oldest breeders of Pugs in the British Isles are Harry and Lou Green, owners of the Harloo Kennels in Shropeshire. The Greens, who recently celebrated their Golden Anniversary, had their first Pugs in 1912, but started breeding about 1934.

While severely curtailed with their breeding program during the 1939 to 1946 World War II hostilities, they managed to sustain a worthy line of Pugs in both fawn and black and are considered to be among the most sincere and successful breeders in the country today.

Over the years the Greens have exported Pugs to many lands, including Finland, Australia, South Africa, Sweden, West Germany, France, Spain, Tangiers, Gibraltar, the Netherlands and the United States. Some of their more notable champions since 1950 have been Catherine of Harloo; Harloo Phillip, who earned his title in 1951; Lord Harry of Harloo, in 1953; Impudence of Harloo, in 1963, and exported to Mrs. Grayson in Harrisburg, Pennsylvania; and the same year Ted's Boy, a fawn that earned his Australian championship when exported to Mrs. W. Gray in New South Wales. In 1959 Mrs. Lee Fahey of Kansas City, Missouri, imported Radium Susie of Harloo, a lovely fawn bitch. A black was the most recent to come to Cincinnati, Ohio, to the Thackers, and earned a championship in this country.

Chapter 2
The Pug in America

The American Kennel Club recognized the Pug Dog in 1885. One Pug was registered that first year. A dog named Roderick stands out in the early history of the breed in this country. An English import, he got off to a bad start at his first show at the Philadelphia Kennel Club Show in 1879 when he was disqualified for carrying his tail on the wrong side! Obviously all three judges at that event were not aware of the old English belief that sex should be denoted by which side the tail curled, and he was carrying it on the distaff side!

At this same show a Pug named Punko, imported by the U.S. Minister to the Court of St. James, emerged the winner. Punko carried his tail on the left! However, Roderick got to do a lot of winning at subsequent shows once all the judges became aware of the breed Standard and the legend about tail carriage had been dispersed.

FIRST IMPORTANT KENNEL

One of the important Pug kennels on the show scene was the Rookery Kennels in Painesville, Ohio. In their ad in the April 3, 1897 issue of the *American Stock-Keeper,* they called themselves "the strongest kennel of sires in America." They called attention to their imports, Finsbury Dong, Finsbury Ding, Ch. Drummer, Finsbury Duke, Challenge Certificate winner Robin Hood, Merry Max and Dave Day. They announced that stud cards and low rates were available upon application and said, "still in the front ranks as importers, breeders and exhibitors."

The Rookery Kennels owned Haughty Madge, an important bitch, whelped on March 15, 1891. Bred to Finsbury Dong, she produced two bitch puppies on July 24, 1894 named Countess Madge and Queen Madge. There is reason to believe that Haughty Madge was also one of the Rookery imports, since a Mr. Bailey of Brighton, England, owned a bitch named Haughty Doris. At any rate, Haughty Madge was one of the first Pugs registered with our American Kennel Club.

Both her Dong daughters were shown, and a write-up on an 1897 Pittsburg dog show in the *American Stock-Keeper* mentioned a report by the judge in a column headed "Mr. James Mortimer's Classes" read as follows:

"PUGS - In open dogs (2) Wallis only loses to Finsbury Duke in body. Bitches (3), Queen Madge, although fat, and Countess Madge, easily scored over Drummer's Satine, while Hooker beat the slightly coarse Robin Hood in Challenge class."

Catalogue listings showed that T. Howard owned Wallis, W.R. Bently owned Satine and a Mr. Howard owned Hooker.

A report on an 1897 Baltimore show, under the heading of Mr. John Brett's Classes, stated: "A small entry, but some of our best were in it. In Challenge dogs it was most close between Robin Hood and Otterburn Treasure, the former has the best head and ear, the other better in legs and color. In bitches Queen Madge and Countess Madge won nicely over Finsbury Duke in head, body and wrinkle. Duttie, while good in body and skill, is long in muzzle, and was again easily beaten by Otterburn Treasure in champion class. Duttie took care of the local class."

At this same show, in the critique for the Miscellaneous Class judged by Mr. T.W. Turner, he wrote: ". . . and Nellie, a big, rough-coated Pug, with a straight-haired curl was third. This was a 'Russian Pug'." Its coat obviously accounted for its being in the Miscellaneous Class rather than with our own Pugs. This may also have been due to probable registration difficulties between Russia and the A.K.C.

COLOR VARIATIONS

The black Pug first appeared in this country around the turn of the century. However, neither they nor the pure white or the pepper and salt colors became popular.

Around 1940 the blacks were pioneered in earnest by Mrs. Florence Bartels with substantial support from Dr. Nancy Riser, the Fred Greenlys, Dr. Stubbs and the John Madores.

THE FAMOUS SIGVALE KENNELS

One of the earliest and finest Pug kennels was Mrs. Sarah Given Waller's Sigvale Kennels in Libertyville, Illinois, opened in 1928. Mrs. Waller was determined to bring the Pug back to the popularity it enjoyed around the turn of the century. The Sigvale Kennels housed about one hundred Pugs and it was not uncommon for Mrs. Waller to bring anywhere from fifteen to twenty entries to the shows to help establish the breed!

Westminster at 8 months of age! She was owned and shown by Mrs. Frothingham Wagstaff.

PUGS IN THE 1930's

Mr. and Mrs. D.F. Petitpain, formerly Boston Terrier enthusiasts, started off the 1930's by doing a lot of winning with Budworth Bombardier. The dog was Best of Winners and Best of Breed at the 1932 New Orleans Kennel Club Show and Group Second. This was one of the best show wins for the breed up to this time, and especially in that part of the country.

Dr. Aristine Pixley Munn of West Long Branch, New Jersey, was winning with Ch. Spring Tide of Broadway, and Miss Louise Poindexter of West Norfolk, Virginia, was breeding Pug dogs at her Love's Point Kennels during this decade. Three of her Pugs were named Rough, Tough and Nasty, contrary to what the kennel name implied. Mr. and Mrs. William R. Baker also had their Wil-Bak Kennels in Norfolk during this period.

Happiness is . . . A passel of Pugs! This is a litter out of Virginia Green's Ch. Meri X-mas Chuckie v Bogin.

Left: Eight-year-old Jackie Ermlich and pal, puppy Paragon's Curiosity Shop. This photo was featured in the *Cincinnati Enquirer* in 1975 to announce the Memorial Day dog shows. **Below:** Le Petite Caporal Napoleon, owned by Mr. and Mrs. Paul G. Sauerwein of New York. Napoleon's recent wins include Best of Winners at the Progressive Dog Club Show. Sire was Ch. Shirrayne's Golddigger ex Fabulous Fifi. Photo by Giovanni Rabidi.

Ch. Blaylock's Katrinka, owned and handled by Hazel M. Martens of San Diego, California. Katrinka finished her championship with five majors under five all-'rounders. This Joan Ludwig photograph was taken in 1964.

THE FIRST PUG DOG CLUB

It was during 1931 that a small band of Pug enthusiasts got together to form the first Pug dog club. They held their first show in conjunction with the 1937 Morris & Essex Show in Madison, New Jersey. However, during the subsequent years the club petered out and there was no new club for the breed until the 1950's when the Pug Dog Club of America was destined to become the parent organization for the breed.

PUGS IN THE 1940's

The Torch of Redgate was still being shown in 1940, owned then by Mrs. Frothingham Wagstaff; he was in fact, a star attraction at the 1940 Progressive Toy Dog show in New York City. Mrs. Frank Downing's Ch. Pride of Ellerslie was winning handsomely at the beginning of this decade, as was Mrs. James Austin's black, Ch. Rochester of Catawba.

The Catawba Kennels were important in the fancy. Known for many breeds of dogs, Pekingese especially, the Catawba Kennels acquired the famous Ch. Diamond Jim from James Trullinger when he dispersed his kennels prior to going into government service before World War II.

Winning with her Pugs in the early 1940's was Miss Winifred Steggall, whose Winna Pugs were well known in show circles. Her Ch. Winna John Bull was much admired. Her kennels were located in Quebec, Canada, and while transportation during the war years was not always easy, she was prominent on the show scene, and had an international champion Pug named Winna Canadian Capers.

Other active breeders during the first half of the 20th century were Charles F. Groose, whose Paramount Kennels were located in Ashland, Ohio; Edna Hillgamyer had her Gin Rickey Kennels in East St. Louis; Marguerite MacLen had her Lucky Ace Kennels in Waterville, New York; Nettie Simmons' Clavon Kennels were in Newport, Rhode Island; and Jane M. Turner was active in Pugs in Torrence, California.

Two other very early breeders that were successful for almost three decades were Al Eberhardt of Camp Dennison, Ohio, and Mrs. L.C. Smith of Long Beach, California, whose Cupid kennel prefix became well known.

The aforementioned James Trullinger's dogs were also popular during these times and remain so today. His Ch. Diamond Jim was Best of Breed at Westminster in 1940. For many years Jim has been a member of the Board of Directors of the Pug Dog Club of America and has served the club in many capacities. In addition to his breeding and exhibiting Pugs in the past several decades, Jim is an all breed judge and continues to keep active in Pug activities today. He is also the author of a book on Pugs. Another of his well-known Pugs was Ch. Puggville's Butcher Boy.

THE SECOND HALF OF THE 20TH CENTURY

While Pugs were making steady and impressive gains during those early years, it was during the 1950's that the breed really caught on and became a popular, established breed in the fancy. There was the continuing success of Mrs. Filomena Doherty's famous Pugville Kennels in Bernardsville, New Jersey. The home of countless fine, top-winning Pugs, Pugville will probably be best

Not So Simpel Simon, owned by Mrs. Phoebe Springall of Devon, England.

Ch. Ivanwold Apple Jack is pictured finishing for championship under judge Alfred E. Treen at the 1976 Okaloosa Kennel Club show. The sire was Ch. Ivanwold Johnny Appleseed ex Ch. Ivanwold High Barbary. Owners are Dr. and Mrs. Edward Patterson of Destin, Florida.

remembered for the incomparable American, Canadian, Cuban and Bermudian Ch. Pugville's Mighty Jim. This potent sire of 38 champions claimed the greatest all-round record for the breed during his lifetime.

At the time of his retirement from the show ring Mighty Jim's record stood at 8 Bests In Show, 65 Group Firsts (including Westminster and Morris & Essex), two Best American-bred In Show, 90 Group Placements and 172 Bests of Breed out of 182 times shown. The Best of Breed wins included four consecutive wins at Westminster, and two at M & E. He was also awarded Best Stud Dog wins in five consecutive specialty shows held by the Pug Dog Club of America.

Mrs. Doherty will also be remembered for her Pugs that gained so much popular recognition for the breed when they were owned by famous people. Princess Grace and Prince Rainier of Monaco have owned a Pugville Pug! The Duke and Duchess of Windsor owned Pugville Pugs! The Windsors have always loved the breed and had several in residence at all times, including several blacks. They both adored Ch. Pugville's Imperial Imp II. There were many other socialites and theatrical people who owned Pugville Pugs during the years.

OTHER PUG GREATS FROM THE 1950's

The 1950's also produced American and Canadian Ch. Blaylock's Mar-Ma-Duke, sire of 26 champions, and Ch. Pugholm's Peter Punkin Eater, sire of 18 champions and #8 in the Toy Group for 1958. Peter was bred and owned by Mr. and Mrs. Frederic Soderberg of Albany, New York, and was a Best In Show winner with 15 Group Firsts and 8 Group Placements.

Gordon Winders of Rochelle, Illinois, owned Mar-Ma-Duke, who placed in the Top Ten Toy Dogs Group in 1957, 1958, 1960 and 1961, and had 13 all-breed Bests In Show to his credit with 62 Group Firsts and innumerable Group Placements during his show ring career. He held the title of "the winningest Pug of all time" during his campaigning. He was bred by Mrs. Rolla Blaylock and handled by Jack Funk.

It was 1950 when Elizabeth and Frederic Soderberg of Albany, New York came upon the scene and established their Pugholm kennels. They bought their first Pug as a pet, but after he won the breed from the classes at his first show at the 1950 Bronx County Show under judge Anna Katherine Nicholas they knew they had a winner. His name was Ch. Wee Hu Spunk. Spunky was later handled by Tom Gately during his ring career. Even more important than his winning at the shows was the fame accorded his son, Ch. Pugholm Peter Punkin Eater, a Best In Show winner and one of the all-time top sires in the breed. He was also the third Pug to win a Toy Group at Westminster. In turn, his son, Ch. Fi Fo, was a breed winner at Westminster, and his son, Ch. Belcrest Jim Dandy, made it three generations of Westminster Best of Breed winners for the Soderberg's kennel!

THE PARENT CLUB

It was early in the 1950's—the exact date is not known—that a club was formed which was to serve from that moment on as the parent organization for the breed. It was called the Pug Dog Club of America and was formed in New York City with an illustrious roster of important people in Pugs up to that time.

The early membership list shows names like Dr. Nancy Riser and Filomena Doherty, etc., as previously mentioned. The first half of the fifties saw other prominent people join the club ranks. Suzanne Bellinger, later Mrs. Joseph Rowe, with the Belcrest

The Duke and Duchess of Windsor and one of their Pug dogs, The Imp, stop in to see the Annual Exhibition Dog Show at the Manhattan Savings Bank. Greeting them is Mr. Willard K. Denton, then president and chairman of the board of the bank, and sponsor of the dog show.

prefix; Ralph Adair; Agnes Miner; Dr. James Stubbs; Mrs. Miriam Koch; Mary Lou Mann of Bee Branch Meadow; Mr. and Mrs. John Madore of Kobby Knoll; and J. Hartley Mellick, Jr., who served as the club's delegate to the American Kennel Club until he moved from New York to Virginia.

By 1956 the club boasted 71 members. Filomena Doherty was serving as president, with John Marsh, Dr. Riser, Jim Trullinger and Walter Foster serving on the board and as officers of the clubs. New names were appearing in the breed, such as John Lavery; Louise Gore, who joined the club in 1957; Mrs. Florence Gamburg; James Geddes; Mrs. Florwina Perry; Marjorie May; and in 1958, Mary Howard, later Mrs. Edwin Pickhardt, was voted to the board. Her Sabbaday Kennels were already famous for a line of excellent Pug dogs that were to dominate in the breed for decades to come.

PUGS IN THE 1960's

Pugs continued to hold their own at the start of the 1960's. The club welcomed Mrs. Lee Fahey; Dr. Harry Smith, Jr., who later became a judge as well as exhibitor; Edwin Rickhardt; John Pratt; Harvey Gregg; Miss Margaret Wells; Mrs. Mary Warner; Tom and Loretta Okun; and Richard Paisley. Other fanciers were Helen Hofstra; judge Mildred Heald; Gunnell Porterfield; Dr. and Mrs. O. Franklin Heisley, who were to campaign their Ch. Pamajo's Kris Kringle; Mr. and Mrs. William T. Braley; Dorothy Fitzpatrick; Herman Gore; and James A. Farrell, Jr.

The second half of the 1960's saw other club members joining the fancy. Margery Shriver, Mr. and Mrs. William Wall, Cecilia Geary, Joan Alexander, Pat Scully, R.D. Hutchinson, Mr. and Mrs. H.L. Benninger, Irene Cartier, Patricia Neidig, Darlene Koch and Russell Hicks were all active in the breed. Mr. and Mrs. Jack Heller were the proud owners of Am., Can. and Mex. Ch. Laja's Blastoff Duke.

1966 also saw the shiny black Pugs of actress Sylvia Sidney enter the show rings. Shown for her by Jane Lamarine, Miss Sidney's Ch. Pug Pen's Captain Midnight was one of several of her winners in subsequent years. Another was her Ch. Captains Kidd. Sylvia Sidney brought additional acclaim to the breed through her needlework. An outstanding artist with needle and thread, she designed and executed many intricate and unbelievably beautiful canvases featuring Pugs. She featured these designs in the several books on needlework that she has had published.

When mentioning the success of handler Jane Lamarine we must also include the name of her young daughter Polly, who, at a very early age, became a handler of Pugs bearing her own kennel name of Silvertown. For many years her name has also appeared as breeder, owner, and exhibitor on a long line of top-winning show Pugs.

PUG WINNERS IN THE 1960's

The #1 Pug for 1966 was an excellent bitch, American and Canadian Ch. Cappoquin Kewpie Doll, owned by Peter and Carolyn Standish of Sewickley, Pennsylvania. Kewpie was also #1 Pug in Canada for the same year, according to the point system compiled by *Dogs In Canada* magazine. All this was accomplished in the same year she completed her championship!

A close second to Kewpie Doll, with 1,256 after Kewpie's 1,476 points, was Ch. Belcrests Jim Dandy. The #3 through #10 pugs were Ch. Pug O My Hearts Vandal, Ch. Bassetts Dapper Dan of Gore, Ch. Crowells Sincerely, Ch. Frolickin Fahey, Ch. Sabbaday Bonanza, Ch. Prillys Rolly Roister, Ch. Hedlunds Jimijon and Ch. Dandys Marco Velvet.

The 1966 Pug Dog Club of America Specialty Show was the main event of the year, and extra "special" perhaps because the judge was Mrs. C.L. Rigden from New Zealand who drew an entry of over 100 Pugs! Her Best of Breed winner was Richard Paisley's bitch, Ch. Staina. Her Best of Opposite Sex went to Ch. Pugville's Bashville Beau, owned by John Pratt.

This specialty also was extra special because it was the first year the club featured a futurity competition. The judge was James W. Trullinger and from the 21 entries he selected two blacks, a brother and sister pair bred by Mrs. Louise Gore. These winners were Smith's Tar Baby of Gore, owned by Doris and Harry Smith, and Gore's Gabrielle, owned by Louise Gore herself.

As a matter of fact, Pugs were winning nicely all over the United States during the second half of the 1960's. Kris Kringle and John Peel were winning in the Northwest, Drum Major on the West Coast, Wolf's Li'l Joe in the Midwest and Little Joe of Gore in the

Actress Sylvia Sidney on her way to a rehearsal with her ever-present Pugs and her sewing bag! Photo by *The Evening Bulletin*, Philadelphia.

Ch. Moran's Masked Marvel, owned by Mr. and Mrs. James Moran of Portland, Oregon. "Poco" is a multi-Group winner and had six Group Placements to his credit in 1976 which will probably put him in the listings of the Top Ten.

Southeast. Mrs. Ann Crowell of Franklin, Tennessee, owned Ch. Crowell's Little Joe of Gore, and was pleased with the tremendous record he had racked up during the first fourteen months of his life! In 1968 on March 23rd he completed his championship. On April 28th he went Best In Show over 917 dogs under judge Mildred Heald and Joe Tacker at the Toledo, Ohio show. On May 5th he was Best In Show again at Lexington, Kentucky. He also had Best of Breed and Group wins to his credit. These wins and the story about Little Joe appeared in the June, 1968 issue of *Popular Dogs* magazine!

During 1968 a French Bulldog and Airedale enthusiast, Mrs. John Butler Prizer of Philadelphia, had branched out into yet another breed. She was showing her beautiful Pug, Sabbaday Springtime Fancy, along with her other dogs at the shows.

The mid-sixties were also the years when Shirley and Rayne Thomas established their Shirrayne Kennels. Originally in Labrador Retrievers, the Thomases became devoted to Pugs.

Shirley has shown many to championships and has sold many to others to be the foundation of their kennels. Shirley has always been dedicated to club activities and has served in many capacities for the breed since joining the PDCA in 1968. She recently sold her Ch. Shirrayne's Golddigger to Tracy Williams from Brazil, but still uses "Golddigger" as her CB radio handle! She now concentrates on showing Ch. Shirrayne's Music Man, co-owned with Carol and Fred Schmidt, to numerous wins. One of his most important wins to date was being Best of Breed at the 1977 Great Lakes Pug Dog Club Specialty. It was a double victory that day when Shirrayne's Tigress Twiggy won the Best In Sweepstakes title.

Four Goodchance Pugs at the home of their owner, Mrs. E.S. Brown in Middlesex, England. Left to right are Goodchance Catherina, Wilhelmina, Delila, and Pyramida. This group, representing three generations of Goodchance Pugs, has done its share of show winning, and has the great distinction of having appeared on British television. Delila appeared with Richard Burton in "The Gathering Storm," Pyramida appeared in "Jenny," the story of the life of Sir Winston Churchill's mother, Catherina appeared in the film "The Great Gatsby" and Wilhelmina, now 11½ years old, appeared in the television play called "The Snares of Death."

During the second half of the 1960's Helen Bearce, Florence Green, Marion Adair, Hazel Wignovich, David Miller, Brenda Baldwin, Peter and Polly McLaughlin and James Cavallaro joined the parent club. Joe Mellor was showing Ch. Auburndale Aquarius, and Hazel Martens attained her membership in the club and eventually gained fame with her Ch. Miller's Imperial Drum Major. Shirley Limoges from Canada was accepted into the club, as was Joseph Rowe, Mark Davis, Mrs. Cleta Chase, Joan Perry, Mr. and Mrs. W.J. Peer, Mr. and Mrs. Paul Plevack and Miss Glen Wells.

By 1968 there were five affiliated clubs around the country and the parent club membership continued to grow. Mrs. Romola

Shirrayne's Hong Kong Jade East, owned by the author, is pictured winning a 3-point major at her first show under judge Ruth Turner at the 1974 Progressive Dog Club show in New York City. Jade, bred by the Shirrayne Kennels, was sired by Ch. Roualyn Shere Khan ex Ch. Greentubs Busy Bee. She was also Best of Opposite Sex at this same show. A Shafer photograph.

1974 Dam of the Year for the Tampa Bay Pug Club was Madam Blossom, owned by Harper's Pugs, Jacksonville, Florida. Blossom has produced four champions from different sires, and one litter of three all achieved their championship.

Hicks, Mrs. Peter Standish, Ruth Freckleton, Mrs. Leola Handlen, Leroy Dougan, George Ensminger, Mrs. Willa Hitt, Mrs. Miles Kelly, Mrs. Victor Gramigna, Harvey Gregg, Rosemarie Knieram, Mrs. Janet Patterson, Jean Prendergast, Helen Snavely, Lorraine Sherwood, Mrs. Bonna Webb, Dr. and Mrs. Robert White and Mr. and Mrs. Glenn Timmons all became members that year.

In 1969 additional members that were to become well known in the breed joined the parent club. Dr. W. Edward McGough, Dr. and Mrs. Arthur Reinitz, Al Meshirer, Marilyn Biggs, Mrs. Ferman Ritter, John Aquino, Barbara Minella, Irene Myette, Ed Pat-

American and Canadian Ch. Wolf's Li'l Joe is pictured in 1967 in an informal "at home" photo. This Top Sire in the history of the breed, with 67 champion get to his credit, has done much to endear the breed to the public by his personality and show record. Bred and owned by Esther Wolf, Omaha, Nebraska. This magnificent specimen will surely go down in the history of the breed as a legend.

terson, Rayne Thomas, Lucille Fichter, Linda Kapsa and Myrtle Landry were among them.

At the board of director's meeting that year it was revealed that the treasury was now in excess of five thousand dollars. This was an interesting comparison to the first treasury report listing $286.33 in the coffers as of February 10, 1950! The club membership now totaled over 250 and additional members were voted in at the April meeting. During the latter part of the year applications for membership were accepted from Mrs. Garnett Gooch, Mrs. Anne Blake James, Carolyn C. Sullivan, Mrs. Sybil T. LeBoeuf, Mrs. Myrna Hasman, Colonel and Mrs. A.R. Green, Pamela Weaver, Rix D. Perkins, Mrs. Gunnell Potterfield, Madeline Van Dyke, John Pomaro and Dr. Ben Johnson.

The latter half of the 1960's was also the time one of the greatest Pugs in the history of the breed was starting his climb up the ladder of success. His name was Ch. Wolf's Li'l Joe. . . .

CH. WOLF'S LI'L JOE

One of the Pug greats that will go down in history as both a top show dog and prepotent sire is Esther and Gus Wolf's American and Canadian Ch. Wolf's Li'l Joe. Joe was top Pug sire for two years in a row, and tied for Top Sire of the Year, all breeds, for 1970. Joe has sired 32 champions and his show record at the end of 1971 was 5 Bests In Show, 122 Bests of Breed, 41 Group Firsts and 111 Group Placements.

In 1970 he ranked #4 in the Phillips System ratings of Top Ten Pugs in the nation, with his grandson, Ch. Top Speed of Even So, in the #2 spot and his son, Ch. Kauffee Royal Brandy Wine, #3. He was #5 in 1971 and #2 in Canada.

For many years Esther Wolf was Pug columnist for *Popular Dogs* magazine, and active in all forms of Pug club work. Both she and Gus are multiple breed judges and reside in Omaha, Nebraska.

Wolf's Li'l Joe won Best In Show at the Sioux City, Iowa, show on September 19, 1971 under judge Ruth Tongren, and was retired on the spot. It was his fifth Best In Show win. His Group win under Rutledge Gilliland that day broke the tie that gave Joe the most Group First wins of any living Pug to that date. He further distinguished himself on this occasion—when his lead broke during the gaiting for Best In Show and Joe continued right down the mat without Esther and went into a perfect show stance in front of the judge! What a superb finish to his sparkling career!

TOP PRODUCING PUG BITCHES

In 1970, the same year Wolf's Li'l Joe tied for Top Producing Sire all-breeds, we had three top-producing Pug bitches to be proud of. Ch. Kauffee Royal Gemini whelped five champion offspring, three of them in 1970. Both litters were sired by L'il Joe. She was whelped in May, 1965, and owned by Mr. and Mrs. Leo Kauffman.

Canadian Ch. Dougan's Darling Dreamer produced four champions from two litters in 1970. She was owned by Mrs. Miles F. Kelley. Hazel Marten's Blaylock Amy whelped four champions, three of them in 1970.

THE 1970's

Pugs were still gaining in popularity as the 1970's got under-

American and Canadian Ch. Wolf's Li'l Joe, Top Show dog and Top Pug Sire in the world, with 67 champion offspring to his credit! This is a record which will probably stand forever more! He has been on the Top Producers list for eight consecutive years with too many champion grandchildren and great grandchildren for his owner to keep track of. At 11 years of age in 1976, Joe was still siring. All during his outstanding career he was handled by owner Esther Wolf of Omaha, Nebraska. He is undeniably one of the most important dogs in the history of the breed!

way. Ch. Heritage Tom Cat of Gore, owned by Barbara Minella of Pinellas, Florida, was #1 dog that year according to *Popular Dogs* magazine's Phillips System awards. Five Group Firsts, an all-breed Best In Show, and 12 Group Placements earned Tom Cat just under three thousand points to earn him the title of top Pug in the country.

It was also in 1970 that Ch. Top Speed of Even So won an all-breed Best In Show. Owned by Agnes Miner of Lakewood, Colorado, this feisty Wolf's Li'l Joe grandson amassed over two thousand Phillips System points from his two Group Firsts and 11 Group Placements. He and Tom Cat were the only two Pugs in the nation to win a Best In Show in 1970 and must be complimented on their success in getting the breed off to a good start.

Seven other Pugs won Groups in 1970, however, which earned them a place in the Top Ten ratings. Ch. Kauffee Royal Brandy

A clean sweep for the the Rowann Kennel blacks! At the 1969 Rapid City Kennel Club show judge Phil Marsh awarded Delilah of Rowann Winners Bitch (and her championship), Rowann's Thumper was Best of Winners and Best of Breed for his championship and went on to Group Second, and American and Canadian Ch. Rowann's Nip of Koal, C.D., was Best of Opposite Sex.

Wine, owned by H. Jacobberge of Omaha, Nebraska, was #3 Pug; his sire, the famous Ch. Wolf's Li'l Joe was #4, having won four Groups and 8 Group Placements out of 16 times shown. Other Group winners were the *#5* Pug, Ch. De Youngs Fancy Free, and the Belcrest Kennel's Ch. Belcrests Aristocratic, who had two Group First and 12 Group Placements. Richard Paisley's Ch. Martlesham Galahad of Bournle won a Group and 6 Group Placements to make him the #7 Pug for this year, with over a thousand Phillips System points.

Ch. Gores Jack Tarr, owned by Mr. and Mrs. R. Hicks of Houston, Texas, was #8 Pug, with two Group Firsts and four Group Placements. Mr. and Mrs. J. Mattos of Salinas, California, owned the #9 Pug and Group winner. Their Ch. Odalisques Cardinal Sin also had four Group Placements. Ch. Miller's Imperial Drum Major, owned by Hazel Martens of Webster, New York, was #10 Pug for 1970 with four Group Placements.

The Joseph Rowe's Ch. Belcrest Aristocratic took the #1 position in the nation's Top Ten in 1972 and again in 1973. Tom Cat had dropped to the #4 position in 1972, and some new names were

All-champion litter whelped by Int. Ch. Pugholms Little Betty Blue pictured with her 10-week-old puppies. She was the dam of eight champions, and this litter was sired by International Champion Bill's Boy of Larimar. Bred by Hazel Martens, Larimar Ranch Kennels, San Diego, California.

Siesta for Wally Provost of Omaha and his Pug, Li'l Dixie Belle. Bred by the Donaldsons of Garnette, Kansas.

appearing on the Top Ten lists. In 1972 Ch. Anchorage Matthew, owned by M. Weissman was #2; Ch. Higman's Little Heller, owned by Mr. and Mrs. R.J. Higman was #3; Mrs. Fahey's Ch. Mi Mis Handsome Harry of Doray was #5; Ch. Blaylocks Rollicking Rollo, owned by J. Martens was #6; Ch. Ellis Dollar Jackpot, #7, was owned by M. Ellis and C. Jackson; the R. Hick's Ch. Hick's Copi Cat was #8. Ch. Angels Ace Hi of Carol Mar co-owned by I.C. Heisley and B.M. Spencer, and Ch. Neubraa Papageno, owned by Richard Paisley, were #9 and #10 respectively.

While Ch. Belcrest's Aristocratic held the #1 spot for 1973, there were two other changes. Ch. Anchorage Matthew dropped from the second spot to #3 and Ch. Mi Mis Handsome Harray of Doray moved from #5 up to #4. All seven other Pugs were newcomers to the list: Ch. Peers Audie, owned by M. Peer, in the #2 position; Ch. Conjours Tuff Jorgell Do It, #5, owned by B.M. Webb and Doug Huffman; Ch. Nunnally's Yield Right Away, owned by Sunmark Kennels and B. Nunnally, #6; Ch. Ivanwold's High Tor, owned by J.K. Patterson, #7; Ch. Mitchell's Alysius,

English Champion Phantasia of Paramin, owned by Mrs. Margo Raisin of Yorkshire, England. Pictured here at the Crufts show, Phantasia has seven CC's, six Reserve CC's and Toy Group Placements.

Mo Jo's Spritely Muggins, owned by Ronald Westall of Washington.

Kendoric's Hazelbridge Eros, photographed in 1976. The sire was Ch. Hazelbridge Black Eros ex Silvertown Onyx. Owned by Doris Aldrich of Pelham, Massachusetts.

owned by A.I. Mitchell, #8; Ch. Fahey's Friendly, owned by Mrs. L. Fahey, #9; and C.R. and N. Nune's Ch. Char Milys Rout About Harri was #10.

WINNING PUGS IN THE MID-1970's

The winning Pug dogs in 1975, as published in *Showdogs* magazine, were: #1-Ch. Chens A Favorite of the Gods, #2-Ch. Faheys Friendly, #3-Ch. Sheffields Dancing Tiger, #4-Ch. Paulaines Wee Ping A Dandy, #5-Ch. Peers Audie, #6-Ch. Shirraynes Golddigger, #7-Broughcastl Balladeer, #8-Ch. Laughing Waters Black Demon, #9-Ch. Jolley Li'l Mojo Sachjon, #10-Ch. Bonjors Tuff Jorgell Do It.

THE GREAT GOLDDIGGER

An American girl in her early twenties living in Sao Paulo, Brazil, got into Pugs the hard way. . . she was thrown from a horse during a show. When the horse fell he broke his back and had to be destroyed; his young owner vowed she would never jump

Ch. Hedlund's Ebony Koal, owned by the Rowann Kennels, Lincoln, Nebraska.

Am., Braz. Ch. Shirrayne's Golddigger, winning at a show in Brazil with his handler, Jayme Martinelli. This Pug was in the Top Ten for 1975, and in four months of showing in Brazil has four Best in Show and six Group Firsts. His American record stands at 34 Bests of Breed, a Group First, nine Group Thirds and four Group Fourths. He is also a Best of Breed winner at the Pug Dog Club of America Specialty show. Owned by Tracy Williams of Sao Paulo, Brazil.

again, even though she had ridden with a Brazilian team in international competition.

Another girl on the team had Pug dogs and when she saw Tracy Williams' distress at losing her horse, she gave her an 8-week-old puppy. It made such a hit that Tracy's mother flew to New York and bought her a black bitch. A black and another fawn dog came soon after, and Tracy Williams was "in the breed!"

At the 1975 Westminster Kennel Club Show Tracy saw Shirley Thomas's Ch. Shirrayne's Golddigger. Even though he was one of Mrs. Thomas's favorites, Tracy managed to buy him from her.

American and Canadian Ch. Rowann's Thumper, a beautiful black Pug owned by the Rowann Kennels of Dr. and Mrs. White of Lincoln, Nebraska. The sire was Am. and Can. Ch. Bombus Black Twig O Tuss ex Am. and Can. Ch. Rowann's Nip of Koal, C.D.

Ch. Cerrone's Johnny Appleseed pictured winning at a 1972 show under respected judge Joseph Rowe. Owned by Dorothy Cerrone of Johnstown, New York.

When they returned to Brazil, Tracy turned Golddigger over to Brazil's top handler, Jayne Martinelli, and at his first show in that country won Best In Show. It was the first time a Pug had ever won Best In Show in that country. At his second and third shows, Digger won the Groups. At his fourth show, Brazil's Dog Festival, he was Best In Show again. He has four top awards so far.

Tracy Williams claims more thrills from winning with the dogs than she ever got from the horses. She must be credited with establishing the breed in that country. Since Digger has been winning, Tracy has had many requests for puppies. These will undoubtedly become the foundations for other kennels in that country.

Golddigger was #5 Pug in the nation for 1975, according to *Showdogs* magazine, before leaving for his new "home country." He can be credited for opening up another horizon for our breed in another country as Pugs continue to gain in popularity as we approach the 1980's!

Chapter 3
Standard For
The Breed

One of the chief functions of the Pug Dog Club of America Inc. is the writing—and, when needed, the periodic revising of the official breed standard. This written depiction of the breed, which is approved by the American Kennel Club, serves to define the "perfect" Pug specimen, and that which is strived for by every conscientious breeder.

If you plan to show your Pug, the standard will be all the more important to you, as you'll use it as a means of appraising your own dog, and to estimate his chances for winning in the show ring.

Symmetry: Symmetry and general appearance, decidedly square and cobby. A lean, leggy Pug and a dog with short legs and long body are equally objectionable.

Size and Condition: The Pug should be *multum in parvo,* but this condensation (if the word may be used) should be shown by compactness of form, well-knit proportions, and hardness of developed muscle. Weight from 14 to 18 pounds (dog or bitch) desirable.

Body: Short and cobby, wide in chest and well ribbed up.

Legs: Very strong, straight, of moderate length and well under.

Feet: Neither so long as the foot of the hare, nor so round as that of the cat; well-split-up toes, and the nails black.

Muzzle: Short, blunt, square, but not up-faced.

Head: Large, massive, round—not apple-headed, with no indentation of the skull.

Eyes: Dark in color, very large, bold and prominent, globular in shape, soft and solicitous in expression, very lustrous, and when excited, full of fire.

Ears: Thin, small, soft, like black velvet. There are two kinds—the "rose" and "button." Preference is given to the latter.

Markings: Clearly defined. The muzzle or mask, ears, moles on cheeks, thumb mark or diamond on forehead, back-trace should be as black as possible.

Mask: The mask should be black. The more intense and well defined it is the better.

Trace: A black line extending from the occiput to the tail.

Wrinkles: Large and deep.

Tail: Curled tightly as possible over the hip. The double curl is perfection.

Coat: Fine, smooth, soft, short and glossy, neither hard nor woolly.

Color: Silver or apricot-fawn. Each should be decided, to make the contrast complete between the color and the trace and the mask. Black.

Scale of Points

	Fawn	Black
Symmetry	10	10
Size	5	10
Condition	5	5
Body	10	10
Legs and feet	5	5
Head	5	5
Muzzle	10	10
Ears	5	5
Eyes	10	10
Mask	5	—
Wrinkles	5	5
Tail	10	10
Trace	5	—
Coat	5	5
Color	5	10
TOTAL	100	100

Chapter 4

Temperament
and
Characteristics

THE PUG PERSONALITY

Far too many people believe that the name Pug comes from the word pugnacious. Nothing could be further from the truth. The dictionary defines the word pugnacious as meaning "quarrelsome" and "inclined to fight." Anyone who has ever owned a Pug dog knows that those descriptions certainly do not describe the Pug personality!

A Pug will seldom start trouble, and today's Pug is far from being classed as a dog that will initiate a fight. However, once provoked they will usually "hang in there" like the Bulldogs and usually emerge victorious!

Rather than pugnacious, we like to think of the Pug as being unafraid of man or beast. Although sometimes stubborn when it comes to relationships with other dogs or discipline, the Pug's general demeanor is far more likely to be described as inquisitive, companionable, loyal and clownish. Pugs really know how to enjoy life and one of their greatest pleasures is to please and to be with their owners.

The Pug requires almost constant contact with those it loves. A Pug is never happier than when right in the middle of family activities, romping with children, side by side on the front seat of the car, sitting on its master's foot while he shaves or resting its velvet muzzle on his mistress' foot amidst the ruffles of the dressing room vanity while she puts on her make-up each day.

The Pug will always rise to the occasion in greeting visiting dogs with the idea of friendly play and will thoroughly enjoy and fit in with other pets in the home if properly introduced.

Pugnacious? No. More like the *Perfect Pet!*

Up, up and over! This photograph of one of Mariann Johnson's puppies typifies the agility the Pug has in spite of its bulk.

WHAT'S IN A NAME?

The Pug is actually said to have gotten its name from the Latin word *pugnus*, which means fist. Their profiles were said to resemble a clenched fist. Another version of this story is that the word pug means monkey, and since they were said to resemble monkeys the name monkey-dog was applied. Another theory is that the word pug comes from the word "puck" and those of us who have owned Pugs might agree this comes close to fitting their impish personalities. The term "my pugg" has, in the past, meant "my pet", as in a term of great affection.

They have also been referred to as "jug-handled dogs" because their curly tails provide a special kind of "handle", and as "figure eight dogs" because of the figure eight pattern the dog sometimes follows when he wishes to get you to follow him. These are, of course, ways that some people observe their dogs, and fortunately, the simple word Pug has outlasted them all!

In addition to a selection of names for the breed, there was also a time when it was believed that the temperament differed between the two colors. Some people claimed that the black was more outgoing and assertive and the fawn preferred the quiet family life. Here again, for every Pug owner there is probably a theory based on the personality of the individual dogs—and everything depends on how much you allow the Pug to become an integral part of your life!

THE PUG WRINKLE

The exaggerated wrinkle the Pug has above its nose requires special care. The depth of the wrinkle makes it a catch-all for excess food, tears or other discharge from the eyes, and it must be kept clean.

Approximately once a week place your hand over the top of the Pug's head and with your thumb gently pull the fold up toward the top of the head from between the eyes. With a wet cotton pad or tissue, wipe out any residue. Dab a little vaseline on your finger and go over the entire area of the wrinkle. See that a slight trace of

Ch. Ivanwold High Jinks pictured winning a four-point major under Robert Reedy at the 1976 Lehigh Valley show. The Sire was Ch. Broughcastle Balladeer ex Ch. Ivanwold High Barbary. Shown exclusively by his co-owner, Charlotte Patterson, Jinks was bred by John Cobb and Dr. Edward Patterson.

vaseline is left behind to soothe any irritation caused by the cleaning along the entire fold.

The same procedure applies to the smaller wrinkles under the eyes. The Pug should not have any "red staining" on the fur around the eyes if they are properly cared for. Any irritation in this area will cause the dog to scratch itself, leading to further skin irritations and possible danger to the eyes.

PUG EYES

The Pug's large, round, protruding eyes must be given special mention here. In all of the "pop-eyed" breeds injury must be prevented if at all possible, and prepared for at least. Aside from

American and Canadian Ch. Kauffee Royal Li'l Mr. Satchmo, sired by the Great Wolf's Li'l Joe ex Ch. Kauffee Royal Gemini. Mr. Satchmo was whelped in 1968 and was owned by Mr. and Mrs. James Moran of Portland, Oregon.

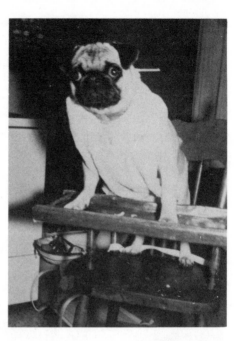

Let's eat! Big John's Jo of Sumner County makes his feelings known. Owned by Mariann Johnson of Enid, Oklahoma.

the normal minor injuries which can occur in any breed, the dogs with the protruding eyes have been known to have their eyes "pop out" of their sockets.

This can be the result of a bump on the head in the area of the eyes, or the result of undue stress (such as squeezing them too hard while restraining them to give medication, cut their nails, clean their teeth, etc.). It is essential to discuss this with your veterinarian and to request a small amount of a pain-killer of some type to keep in your canine medicine cabinet should you have this happen. It is possible in some cases to save the eye if you can get the dog to the veterinarian immediately. It will be necessary, however, to give the dog something to relieve the pain so that it does not do further damage to itself by scratching the eye out entirely. The veterinarian may be able to place the eye back in the socket.

Breeders have been known to accomplish this themselves, but in any event, the dog must see the veterinarian immediately to avoid any further damage and to eliminate the danger of infection.

Check your Pug's eyes daily to see that they are clear of any foreign matter (lint, seeds, dust, etc.) and make a special check

59

Ch. Fiddler Fahey is pictured winning the 1965 Pug Dog Club of America show under Judge Percy Roberts. Presenting the trophy is singer Lena Horne. Fiddler's sire was Fahey's Filbert, and he was bred, owned and handled by Mrs. Lee Fahey of Kansas City, Missouri.

after riding in cars, being at the beach and after bathing or swimming.

A drop of a product called Eye Brite will not only brighten as the name implies, but will clear out the eyes after grooming. This is especially needed by the show dog.

DEW CLAWS

All dew claws should be surgically removed at around two to five days after birth. Being a short-haired dog, the Pug deserves the nice "clean" look of legs free of these hazardous appendages. Where the front legs are concerned, dew claws actually present a danger to the eyes.

The Pug uses its front paws in much the same manner as a

human baby, to rub its eyes, clear its face and to hold onto bones and toys. Since the mouth of the Pug is in such close proximity to the eyes dew claws present a danger if allowed to grow. They also are apt to catch onto things which can impede their walking or running through brush or tall grasses. Dew claws serve no purpose and should therefore be removed.

When done during the first few days of life, this is a relatively simple and painless procedure. If neglected and done later in life, dew claw removal is an actual operation and incurs all the usual risks of other surgery.

"The joy of owning a Pug" could well be the title of this charming photograph of actress Sylvia Sidney and one of her adored black Pugs. Miss Sidney is, in addition to her fame as a needleworker, also an artist of note.

PUG EARS

One of the most important features of the Pug head are those "black velvet ears!" The correct ear set does so much for that desired "typical Pug dog expression!"

To help assure the desired ear set in the mature Pug, Shirley Thomas, well-known breeder and exhibitor of Best In Show Pugs, has devised a method for "gluing" the Pug ears while they are inclined to "fly" during the cutting of their second teeth. This gluing will help train and strengthen the ear muscles so that they will hold their ears correctly at maturity. See page 105 for diagram.

Diagrams and the three necessary steps are included here. It is simple, painless and accomplished with the glue used for adhering womens' false eyelashes. Therefore, this glue is easily removed and safe. Be sure to clean your Pug's ears at least once a week with Q-tips, and especially before a dog show. During the bath place small wads of cotton in them to prevent soap and water from getting down into them.

It is interesting to note that during the nineteenth century many Pugs had their ears cropped off close to their heads. This became the fashion with the ladies that walked their Pugs along the boulevards along with their turbaned Negro pages. They believed the cropping of ears encouraged the desirable wrinkling on their foreheads!

PUG TAILS

Another of the charming features of the Pug dog is the delightful double-curled twisted tail! It should be carried up over the back when the dog is in normal stance or in motion. "At rest" it has been known to uncurl like those children's party favors that unravel when you blow into them!

A curl that is carried off to one side is undesirable and will go against the dog in the show ring, as well as detract from the general appearance.

When you run your fingers through the curl it should feel firm and the characteristic circle should be very much in evidence.

THE PUG TRACE

Around the turn of the century some Pugs had definite black markings across the shoulders. These were called saddle-marks

Fun in the autumn leaves for Ch. Dhandy's English Knickers, owned by Mr. and Mrs. E. G. Willard of Tampa, Florida.

and later referred to as part of the trace. Today's Pug does not always carry or keep a trace, but this darker suggestion of a "stripe" down his back consists of black-tipped hairs and is certainly desirable and thoroughly appealing.

PUG TEETH

Confusion with the exaggerated bite of the Bulldog gave some of the early English fanciers the idea that because of the pushed-in face the Pug's tongue should protrude. Fortunately for the breed this idea was dispelled before too much damage had been done.

While the bite is not "even" and the lower jaw protrudes beyond the upper jaw, the Pug has enough "lip" to cover the teeth and there is no reason at all for the tongue to protrude.

Teeth should be cleaned when and if necessary, usually twice a year. Avoid tartar buildup that will require cleaning under

Three generations of pugs at Doris Aldrich's kennel in Pelham, Massachusetts. Bohemian Joey of Kae-Jac, C.D., Canadian Ch. Kendoric's Li'l China Star, C.D. and Kendoric's Triple Trouble.

anesthesia, since short nosed breeds do not always take well to anesthetics. Good diet and Nylabones® will usually be sufficient to keep teeth clean and gums healthy. Keep several small Nylabones® , available at pet shops, on hand at all times and encourage your pet to chew on them.

DO PUGS SNORE?

The answer, in all honesty, is—sometimes. A lot of factors contribute to the sounds emanating from your Pug when he sleeps.

All breeds with "pug noses" are inclined to snore in varying degrees, but if the Pug face is a good one, with proper nose placement, there should only be occasional circumstances that would cause excessive snoring.

When the Pug becomes highly overheated it pants heavily and will snort or snore when trying to "level off" or calm down. The Pug might snore if humidity is very high, or if a room is too warm or has little air circulation.

Pugs will also snore if they sleep on their backs or snuggle down in the deep folds of covers or blankets. During the normal course of a normal day, the Pug does not snore or snort. If your Pug does snore or snort excessively it should be discussed with your veterinarian as this is a possible indication of some more complicated condition, such as a blockage, allergy, or the symptom of a respiratory disease.

Above: A pair of old German porcelain Pugs and a small French ceramic box with pair of Pugs on top. From the collection of James Moran. **Below:** Four treasured pieces from James Moran's collection. On the left is a Staffordshire Pug; the plate is a Luster-Less glass plate from the American Glass Works, with an oil painting of Pug head, and dated pre-Civil war; a Pug head ceramic bank, a statue of a Pug with a Spitz dog; and an old ceramic figurine.

HEAT PROSTRATION

In the same "breath" with discussing a Pug that snores or snorts because of atmospheric conditions, we come immediately to the subject of their reaction to excessive heat. There is no denying that Pugs do react to the heat and have difficulty breathing during very hot weather. The earliest reactions to the effects of the heat are heavy panting, snorting or gasping.

For those Pugs that live in extremely hot or humid climates, or for those who travel with their owners during the warm weather, it is possible to avoid a crisis by purchasing a child's throat collar, or ice bag, which can be tied around their necks after being filled with ice cubes.

These collars can be purchased at any hospital supply company or store. You ask for a Davol #379 child's throat collar. If they do not have one in stock ask them to order one for you from Davol, Inc., Providence, Rhode Island.

When traveling, carry a large thermos of cold water for occasional small drinks and for saturating towels for the dog to either sit on or be covered with until you reach your destination.

Wiping the face occasionally with a cold, wet face cloth or paper towel will also help keep down body heat, or you can let them lick ice cubes.

Remember to salt the food after heavy panting so that you can help replace the salt or sodium they have "panted away" during exposure. This expelled salt sometimes can be seen as a little white crust on the dog's nose.

Ch. Ritter's Charmin Kelly, dam of four champions, sired by English and American Ch. Phidgity Phircone ex Ch. Drum Major's Bit O'Honey. Owned by Mrs. Ferman Ritter of Sewickley, Pennsylvania.

During normal conditions at home and while traveling the Pug will not require any such special considerations, but it is wise to always be prepared for them.

THE PUG VOICE

Pugs are not barkers per se. They seldom bark without cause, but in the presence of other breeds known to be barkers they will join in, but only after seeming to appraise the situation, or just to be agreeable.

Even when the Pug does bark it is a soft and steady bark, not the shrill kind that "gets on your nerves." More often than not the Pug will "chortle" when someone threatens to take away their toys or if they are frustrated. They sit back on their haunches like little fat elephants, throw their heads back, make a little "o" of their mouths and emit a low "howl." It can barely be heard but it is so soulful and entreating that you find you cannot resist it!

It is this soft, seldom-heard bark that earns the Pug the title of "ideal apartment house dog!" They will bark to let you know someone is coming, but it is never loud enough to bring the neighbors to the point of complaining about it.

THE PUG AS A GUARD AND HUNTING DOG

For the reasons mentioned above regarding their soft, but insistent barking habits, I automatically nominate the Pug as a top guard dog for apartment dwellers! They are easy to keep, quiet, clean, and alert to strangers. If you have a Pug in an apartment and it barks, you would be wise to investigate for the approach of strangers.

For numerous reasons, the Pug has never been classed as a hunting dog. It's a "people" dog and will retrieve nothing more than toys! Viva la difference!

PUG MOVEMENT

When watching the Pug gait one should get the impression of a steady, sure mover. The Pug's power comes from the front, with an almost tracking gait, which is the typical Pug rolling movement. The Pug gait should *never* resemble or be compared to the heavy roll of the Bulldog.

Above: Seeing double? No, Ch. Dhandy's English Knickers and his look-alike son strike one of their favorite poses. Owned by the E.G. Willards of Tampa, Florida. **Right:** Ch. Sabbaday Robin of Udalia, owned by Mrs. James A. Farrel, Jr. of Darien, Connecticut.

Above, left: Ken M's Sugar and Spice, pictured winning at a California show under judge Mrs. Glen Fancy. Handled by breeder-owner Diana Mulhern, Santa Ana, California. **Above, right:** A precious portrait of Mary Bouyear's Donaldson's Muffin Man, bred by Wayne and Marie Donaldson.

BEST OF BREED
SHAFER PHOTO

Left: Ch. Fichter Fay Al Jol Sin Chen pictured winning at the 1975 Greenwich Kennel Club show under judge R. Graham. He is owned by Susan and Gary Karp of Washington, D.C., and handled by Mr. Karp. **Below:** Ch. Li'l Sugar of MSJ is pictured winning a three-point major as Best of Winners and Best Opposite Sex at an Austin, Texas show under Judge D. Nickles. Owner/handler Mariann S. Johnson, Kennel of Pugs, Enid, Oklahoma.

Chapter 5

General Care

Perhaps the most important thing you will ever do for your puppies' good health is to strictly adhere to a schedule of the necessary vaccinations. Taking these precautions is a giant step towards insuring good health and life.

VACCINATIONS

If you are to raise a puppy, or a litter of puppies, successfully, you must adhere to a realistic and strict schedule of vaccination. Many puppyhood diseases can be fatal—all of them are debilitating. According to the latest statistics, 98 per cent of all puppies are being inoculated after 12 weeks of age against the dread distemper, hepatitis and leptospirosis. Most manage to escape these horrible infections. Orphaned puppies should be vaccinated every two weeks until the age of 12 weeks. Distemper and hepatitis live-virus vaccine should be used, since the pups are not protected with the colostrum normally supplied to them through the mother's milk. Puppies weaned at six to seven weeks should also be inoculated repeatedly because they will no longer be receiving mother's milk. While not all will receive protection from the serum at this early age, it should be given and they should be vaccinated once again at both nine and 12 weeks of age.

A leptospirosis vaccination should be given at four months of age, with thought given to booster shots if the disease is known in the area, or in the case of show dogs which are exposed on a regular basis to many dogs from far and wide. While annual boosters are in order for distemper and hepatitis, every two or three years is sufficient for leptospirosis, unless there is an outbreak in your immediate area. The one exception should be the pregnant bitch since there is reason to believe that inoculation might cause damage to the fetus.

Strict observance of such a vaccination schedule will not only keep your dog free of these debilitating diseases, but will prevent

71

Top, left: Ch. Murphy's Little Golden Kelli, pictured winning a 4-point major under judge Mildred Heald at a Tampa, Florida, show. The sire was Ch. Ah Ya Gung Ho Murphy ex Ch. Dandy's Debutante. Owned by Shirley and Pam Tackett of Lutz, Florida. **Top, right:** Ch. Belcrests Jim Dandy, another top-winning Pug dog owned by Joseph and Suzanne Rowe of Scotia, New York. This picture shows Jim Dandy winning the Toy Group at a 1968 show under judge Edith Nash Hellerman, with Roy Holloway handling. **Bottom, left:** Ch. Ken M's O'Shay, bred and owned by Ken and Diana Mulhern of Santa Ana, California, pictured winning Group Second at the 1974 Silver Bay Kennel Club Show under judge Peter Thomson. Handled by Diana Mulhern. **Bottom, right:** American and Canadian Champion Rowann's Happy Ho Tei pictured winning the Toy Group.

Top, left: Ch. Paulaine's Wee Ping-A-Dandy, #1 Pug for Best of Breed wins, 1975 plus #4 Pug in the Phillips System and Kennel Review system the same year. **Top, right:** Ch. Paragon's Little Centurion finished his championship with this 5-point major win under judge Piper. **Bottom, left:** Ch. Susan B. Anthony and Jeff Webb winning under Jane Kay at the 1974 Dayton K.C. Show. **Bottom, right:** Shirrayne's Golden Gaymark wins Best Adult in Match at a 1974 Pug Dog Club of Greater N.Y. show before starting his show career.

an epidemic in your kennel, or in your locality, or to the dogs which are competing at the shows.

Since new serums are constantly being improved and discovered, it is wise to regularly consult your veterinarian for the latest and best kind for your Pug.

WHAT THE THERMOMETER CAN TELL YOU

Practically everything a dog might contract in the way of sickness has basically the same set of symptoms. Loss of appetite, diarrhea, dull eyes, dull coat, warm and/or runny nose and FEVER!

Therefore, it is most advisable to have a thermometer on hand for checking temperature. There are several inexpensive metal rectal-type thermometers that are accurate and safer than the glass variety which can be broken. This may happen either by dropping, or perhaps even breaking off in the dog because of improper insertion or an aggravated condition with the dog that makes him

Ch. Auburndale Aquarius, sire of Ch. Anchorage Matthew and a Group winner himself. This Tauskey photograph shows him at about 13 months of age at the start of his show ring career. Owned by Joe V. Mellor of Sayville, Long Island, New York.

Esther Wolf's Lulu Belle, the great grandmother of Esther's famous Ch. Wolf's Li'l Joe.

violently resist the insertion of the thermometer. Whichever type you use, it should first be sterilized with alcohol and then lubricated with vaseline to make the insertion as easy as possible.

The normal temperature for a dog is 101.5° Fahrenheit, as compared to the human 98.6°. Excitement as well as illness can cause this to vary a degree or two, but any sudden or extensive rise in body temperature must be considered as cause for alarm. Your first indication will be that your dog feels unduly "warm". This is the time to take the temperature, not when the dog becomes very ill or manifests additional serious symptoms.

ASPIRIN: A DANGER

There is a common joke about doctors telling their patients, when they telephone with a complaint, to take an aspirin, go to bed and let them know how things are in the morning. Unfortunately, far too many dog owners think aspirins are cure-alls and give them to their dogs indiscriminately, calling the veterinarian only when the dog has had an unfavorable reaction.

Aspirins are not panaceas, certainly not for every dog. There has been evidence of ulceration in varying degrees on the stomach lin-

75

Top, left: American and Canadian Ch. Ritter's Copper Penny winning under judge Edith Hellerman at a 1974 show. The sire was Ch. Ritter's Travelin Apache ex Ch. Ritter's Charmin Kelly. Bred, owned and handled by Mrs. Ferman Ritter of Sewickley, Pennsylvania. **Top, right:** Best in Show Ch. Sheffield's Dancing Tiger, owned by Mrs. Walter Jeffords and Michael Wolf. Bred by Margery Shriver, the Tiger is shown winning the top award under judge Tipton at the 1976 Lehigh Valley Kennel Club show. Handled by Richard Grillo, the sire was Am., Can. Ch. Wolf's Lil'l Joe ex Am., Can. Ch. Sheffield's Sure-Fire. **Bottom, left:** Ch. Belcrests Aristocratic, top-winning Pug shown with his handler Roy Holloway winning a Toy Group at a Rubber City Kennel Club Show. Aristocratic was in the Top Ten category and broke all records for the breed during his show career. Owned by Joseph and Suzanne Rowe of Scotia, New York. **Bottom, right:** Ch. Wisselwood Raven Soul pictured winning his second Specialty major win from the Puppy Class under judge Suzanne Rowe. Owner-handled by Mrs. Lorene M. Vickers of Beach City, Ohio. The sire was Ch. Tick Tock of LeTasyll ex Wisselwood Touch of Class.

Tosh's Angus of Thorn, owned by Shirley L. Tosh, Wallingford, Conn.

ings when necropsy was performed. Veterinary consultation is required to determine your dog's tolerance to them and the proper dosage.

MASTURBATION

A source of embarrassment to many dog owners, masturbation can be eliminated with a minimum of training.

The dog which is constantly breeding anything and everything, including the leg of the piano or perhaps the leg of your favorite guest, can be broken of the habit by stopping its cause.

The over-sexed dog—if truly that is what he is—which will never be used for breeding can be castrated. The kennel stud dog can be broken of the habit by removing any furniture from his quarters or keeping him on leash and on verbal command when he is around people or in the house where he might be tempted to breed pillows, people, etc.

Hormone imbalance may be another cause and your veterinarian may advise injections. Exercise can be of tremendous help. Keeping the dog's mind occupied by physical play when he is around people will also help relieve the situation.

Females might indulge in sexual abnormalities like masturbation during their heat cycle, or again, because of a hormone imbalance. If they behave this way because of a more serious problem, a hysterectomy may be indicated.

A sharp "no!" command when you can anticipate the act, or a sharp "no!" when caught in the act will deter most dogs if you are consistent in your correction. Hitting or other physical abuse will only confuse a dog.

RABIES

The greatest fear in the dog world today is still the great fear it has always been—rabies!

The only way rabies can be contracted is through the saliva of a rabid animal entering the bloodstream of another animal or person, usually by way of a bite. There is the Pasteur treatment for rabies which is effective if administered immediately after exposure to an affected animal. We now know that the biggest rabies carriers are bats, skunks, foxes, rabbits and other warm-blooded animals that roam free. Pets that are allowed to roam free *must* be inoculated. Most cities provide such inoculations free of charge.

The incubation period for rabies is usually two weeks to six months, and there is no known cure. It leads to a horrible death in both animals and humans, so it is essential that all bites be reported to the health department.

There are two kinds of rabies; one form is called "furious," and the other is referred to as "dumb." The mad dog goes through several stages of the disease. His disposition and behavior change radically and suddenly; he becomes irritable and vicious; the eating habits alter, and he rejects food for things like stones and sticks; he becomes exhausted and drools saliva out of his mouth almost constantly. He may hide in corners, look glassy-eyed and suspicious, bite at the air as he races around snarling and attacking with his tongue hanging out. At this point paralysis sets in, starting at the throat so that he can no longer drink water though he desires it desperately; hence, the term hydrophobia is given. He begins to stagger and eventually convulse, and death is imminent.

In "dumb" rabies paralysis is swift; the dog seeks dark, sheltered places and is abnormally quiet. Paralysis starts with the jaws, spreads down the body and death is quick. Contact by humans or other animals with the drool from either of these types of rabies on open skin can produce the fatal disease, so extreme haste and proper diagnosis is essential. In other words, you do not have to be bitten by a rabid dog to have the virus enter your system. An open wound or cut that comes in touch with the saliva is all that is needed.

Rabies is no respec*er of age, sex or geographical location. It is found all over the world from North Pole to South Pole, and has nothing to do with the old wives' tale of dogs going mad in the hot summer months. True, there is an increase in reported cases during summer, but only because that is the time of the year for animals to roam free in good weather and is the mating season when the battle of the sexes is taking place. Inoculation and a keen eye for symptoms and bites on our dogs and other pets will help control the disease until the cure is found.

Overleaf: Marvelous Pug puppy that grew up to be Am., Can. Ch. Bitterwell Broth of a Boy, owned by the Shirrayne Kennels.

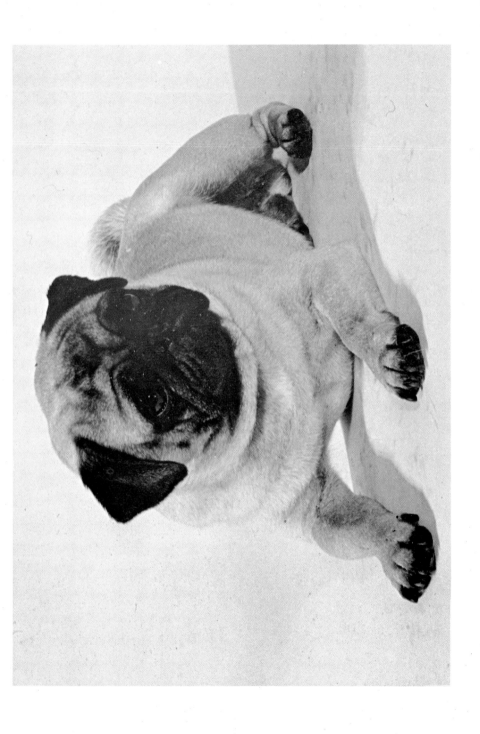

Ch. Bronnie of Martlesham, sired by the 1976 Swedish Best in Show winner, Int. Ch. Bronson of Martlesham. Owned by Nancy Gifford, Martlesham Kennels, Suffolk, England.

TATTOOING

Ninety per cent success has been reported on the return of stolen or lost dogs that have been tattooed. More and more this simple, painless, inexpensive method of positive identification for dogs is being reported all over the United States. Long popular in Canada, along with nose prints, the idea gained interest in this country when dognapping started to soar as unscrupulous people began stealing dogs for resale to research laboratories. Pet dogs that wander off and lost hunting dogs have always been a problem. The success of tattooing has been significant.

Tattooing can be done by the veterinarian for a minor fee. There are several dog "registries" that will record your dog's number and help you locate it should it be lost or stolen. The number of the dog's American Kennel Club registration is most often used on thoroughbred dogs, or the owner's Social Security number in the case of mixed breeds. The best place for the tattoo is the groin. Some prefer the inside of an ear, and the American Kennel Club has rules that the judges officiating at the AKC dog shows should not penalize the dog for the tattoo mark.

The tattoo mark serves not only to identify your dog should it be

Overleaf: Am., Can. Ch. Ritter's Sesame Street, shown winning at a 1974 show under judge Kenneth Miller. The sire was Ch. Ritter's Travelin Apache ex Ch. Ritter's Charmin Kelly. Bred and owned by Mrs. Ferman Ritter.

Ch. Dandy's Marco Velvet, a Group-winning Pug that has been on the lists of Top Ten in the breed. The sire was Ch. Pug-Havens Cactus Pandy ex Ch. Velvet Tracey, C.D. Owned by Mr. and Mrs. William J. Braley.

lost or stolen, but offers positive identification in large kennels where several litters of the same approximate age are on the premises. It is a safety measure against unscrupulous breeders "switching" puppies. For safety's sake, the sooner you tattoo your dog the better.

THE FIRST AID KIT

It would be sheer folly to try to operate a kennel or to keep a dog without providing for certain emergencies that are bound to crop up when there are active dogs around. Just as you would provide a first aid kit for people, you should also provide a first aid kit for the animals on the premises.

The first aid kit should contain the following items:

medicated powder	adhesive tape
jar of petroleum jelly	adhesive bandages
cotton swabs	cotton
bandage-1 inch gauze	boric acid powder

A trip to your veterinarian is always safest, but there are certain preliminaries for cuts and bruises of a minor nature that you can care for yourself.

Overleaf: Waterside Royal Wind Song, C.D., owned by Susan B. Burnham, Waterside Pugs, Cheshire, Conn. Wind Song earned her three legs in three shows as well as 10 points toward championship at the same time.

Cuts, for instance, should be washed out and medicated powder or petroleum jelly applied with a bandage. The lighter the bandage the better so that the most air possible can reach the wound. Cotton swabs can be used for removing debris from the eyes after which a mild solution of boric acid wash can be applied. As for sores, use dry powder on wet sores, and petroleum jelly on dry sores. Use cotton for washing out wounds and drying them.

A particular caution must be given here on bandaging. Make sure that the bandage is not too tight to hamper the dog's circulation. Also, make sure the bandage is made correctly so that the dog does not bite at it trying to get it off. A great deal of damage can be done to a wound by a dog tearing at a bandage to get it off. If you notice the dog is starting to bite at it, do it over or put something on the bandage that smells and tastes bad to him. Make sure, however, that the solution does not soak through the bandage and enter the wound. Sometimes, if it is a leg wound, a sock or stocking slipped on the dog's leg will cover the bandage edges and will also keep it clean.

COPROPHAGY

Perhaps the most unpleasant of all phases of dog owning is to get one that takes to eating stool. This practice, which is known as coprophagy, is one of the unsolved mysteries in the dog world. There simply is no proven explanation to why some dogs do it.

However, there are several logical theories, all or any of which may be the cause. Some say nutritional deficiencies; another says that dogs inclined to gulp their food (which passes through them not entirely digested) find it still partially palatable. There is another theory that the preservatives used in some meat are responsible for an appealing odor that remains through the digestive process. Poor quality meat can be so tough and unchewable that dogs swallow it whole and it passes through them in large undigested chunks.

There are others who believe the habit is strictly psychological, the result of a nervous condition or insecurity. Others believe the

Overleaf: Tosh's Angus of Thorn, owned by Shirley L. Tosh of Wallingford, Connecticut.

The ultimate in housebreaking at Esther Wolf's kennel in Omaha, Nebraska! Actually, the Pug *is* a relatively clean dog who should present no housebreaking difficulties if properly trained.

dog cleans up itself because it is afraid of being punished as it was when it made a mistake on the carpet as a puppy. Others claim boredom is the reason, or even spite. Others will tell you a dog does not want its personal odor on the premises for fear of attracting other hostile animals to itself or its home.

The most logical of all explanations and the one most veterinarians are inclined to accept is that it is a deficiency of dietary enzymes. Too much dry food can be bad and many veterinarians suggest trying meat tenderizers, monosodium glutamate or garlic powder which gives the stool a bad odor and discourages the dog. Yeast or certain vitamins or a complete change of diet are even more often suggested. By the time you try each of the above you will probably discover that the dog has outgrown the habit anyway. However, the condition cannot be ignored if you are to enjoy your dog to the fullest.

There is no set length of time that the problem persists, and the only real cure is to walk the dog on leash, morning and night and after every meal. In other words, set up a definite eating and exercising schedule before coprophagy is an established pattern.

Top, left: Am., Bda., Can. Ch. Revel's Merrymaker, C.D. owner-handler-trainer is Patricia Scully of Suffern, N.Y. **Top, right:** Ch. Crowell's Brass Band winning under Ruth Turner at the 1973 Staten Island K.C. show. **Bottom, left:** Ch. Shirrayne's Cute Cookie winning at the 1972 Hockamock K.C. show. **Bottom, right:** Am., Can. Ch. Sabbaday Favor, going Best of Opposite Sex at the 1974 Chester Valley K.C. show.

Susie Wong, a fawn bitch owned by Phoebe Springall of Devon, England.

DO ALL DOGS CHEW?

Yes! And Pugs are no exception. Chewing is the best possible method of cutting teeth and exercising gums. Every Pug puppy goes through this teething process, and it can be destructive if the puppy uses shoes, table corners or rugs instead of the proper item for the best possible results.

Dried rawhide products of various types, shapes, sizes and prices have come on the market during the past few years. They don't serve the primary chewing functions particularly well, they are a bit messy when wet from mouthing, and most dogs chew them up rather rapidly—but they have been considered safe for dogs until recently. During the past few months, however, a number of cases of death, and near death, by strangulation have been reported to be the result of partially swallowed chunks of rawhide swelling in the throat. More recently some veterinarians have been attributing cases of acute constipation to large pieces of incompletely digested rawhide in the intestine. Nevertheless, in the opinion of this writer, the rawhide products present a lesser danger to dogs than do the cheap plastic and rubber toys and many kinds of natural bones.

The nylon bones, especially those with natural meat and bone fractions added, such as Nylabone®, are probably the most com-

Overleaf: Ch. Donaldson's Li'l Abner and daughter Donaldson's Little Bo Peep winning under breeder-judge Gus Wolf at a recent Midwest show. Bred, owned and handled by Marie and Julie Donaldson of Garnett, Kansas.

plete, safe and economical answer to the chewing need. Dogs cannot break them or bite off sizeable chunks; hence, they are completely safe—and being longer lasting than other things offered for the purpose, they are economical.

Hard chewing raises little bristle-like projections on the surface of the nylon bones—to provide effective interim tooth cleaning and vigorous gum massage, much in the same way your tooth brush does it for you. The little projections are raked off and swallowed in the form of thin shavings—but the chemistry of the nylon is such that they break down in the stomach fluids and pass through without effect.

The toughness of Nylabone® provides the strong chewing resistance needed for important jaw exercise and effective help for the teething functions—but there is no tooth wear because nylon is non-abrasive. Being inert, nylon does not support the growth of microorganisms—and it can be washed in soap and water, or it can be sterilized by boiling or in an autoclave.

When you see your Pug pick up an object to chew, immediately

Ch. Shirrayne's Cool Cappy wins Best of Breed from the classes under judge Geraldine Hess at the 1973 Grand River Kennel Club Show, on the way to his championship. Handler is his breeder-owner, Shirley Thomas, Shirrayne Kennels, Flushing, New York.

Dr. Robert Gossweiler stands in front of one of his original design hooked rugs featuring a Pug dog head. Dr. Gossweiler has done several rugs and wall hangings of our breed.

A wall in Helen Bortner's home in Baltimore, featuring part of her collection of paintings of Pugs. On the extreme right is a curio cabinet containing dozens of Pug figurines.

Above, left: Eagerly awaiting Christmas festivities is Ch. Dhandy's English Knickers, owned by Mr. and Mrs. E.G. Willard of Tampa, Florida. **Above, right:** Can. Ch. Pugtowne's Scooby-Doo, owned by the Pugtowne Kennels, Oceanside, New York. Scooby-Doo also has points toward his American championship.

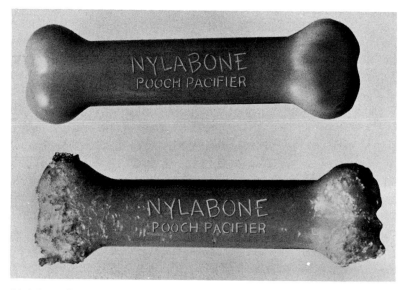

Nylabone®, a unique 100 percent nylon chew bone, is the perfect chewing pacifier for young dogs in their teething stage, or even for older dogs to help satisfy that occasional urge to chew. Unlike many other dog bones on the market today, Nylabone® does not splinter or fall apart. It will last indefinitely and as it is used it frills, becoming a doggie toothbrush that cleans teeth and massages gums.

remove it from his mouth with a sharp "No!" and replace the object with a Nylabone®. Puppies take anything and everything into their mouths so they should be provided with several of them to prevent damage to the household. This same Nylabone® eliminates the need for any other kind of bone which may chip and injure your dog's mouth, stomach or intestinal walls. Cooked bones, soft enough to be powdered and added to the food, are also permissible if you have the patience to prepare them, but Nylabones® serve all the purposes of bones for chewing that your dog may require, so why take a chance on meat bones?

Electrical cords and wires of any kind present a special danger if chewed on. All exposed wires must be eliminated during puppyhood, as should hazardous glass dishes which can be broken and played with.

Chapter 6
Buying Your Pug Puppy

The Secretary of the Pug dog club in your area, the American Kennel Club, or the classified ads in your local newspaper can put you in touch with breeders that have Pugs for sale. It would also be to your advantage to attend a few dog shows where you can talk to exhibitors about buying a Pug. Reading everything you can find about the Pug in dog magazines and books available at pet stores and libraries will also help you make an informed decision.

If you are buying your Pug as a pet buy the one that is healthy and that appeals to you most. However, if you wish to show the dog make certain you buy from a reputable breeder of show Pugs and that you take another Pug "expert" with you if possible. Don't buy the first cute puppy you see, and visit as many kennels as possible before making your decision.

THE PUPPY YOU BUY

A puppy should not leave the mother until it is *at least* 8 weeks old, better still if it's 12 weeks old, at which time it has been wormed and had its first protective inoculation. It should be a clean, active, outgoing puppy and a reputable breeder should be willing to let you have a 24-hour veterinary check-up before finalizing the sale. A deposit or a postdated check is usually agreeable, with the official papers being forwarded after the actual sale. The pedigree should go with the puppy, however.

Have your mind pretty well made up before you begin to look around whether you want a male or female. It will narrow down your selection of puppies and avoid confusion. Check for clean teeth, sweet breath, clear eyes, clean ears, good pink gums, and clear skin. Rub the fur the wrong way to see if there are any signs of fleas, or red blotches that indicate other insects or dietary disturbances. The puppy should be clean, its coat not matted with dry excrement or smelling of urine. It's hard to keep puppies clean, but it can—and should—be done by all breeders! And check

Above: Ravencrofts Nimrod of Kae-Jac, owned by Shirley L. Tosh of Wallingford, Connecticut. **Below:** Some valuable bronzes of Pugs from Helen Bortner's tremendous collection. Several illuminated curio cabinets contain hundreds of priceless pieces.

Shirrayne's Sassy Sandia, photographed in September 1976 when she was just eight weeks old. Owner, A. Paul of Howard Beach, New York.

Ch. Ah-Ya Irish Penny, top-winning bitch co-owned by Mrs. R.D. Hutchinson and Mrs. W.J. Braley of Tampa, Florida.

Am., Can., Cuban, Bda. Ch. Pugville's Mighty Jim, owner Filomena Doherty, Wash. Crossing, Pa. Whelped in 1950, he was the pride of Pugville Kennels when he died in 1965.

Above: A litter of Pugs bred several years ago by Mr. and Mrs. Edgar Messenger of Oklahoma City, Oklahoma. **Left:** A five-day old Pug puppy at the Ivanwold Kennels in Destin, Florida. **Below:** The Pug puppy that was greatly responsible for the author getting interested in the breed . . . bred by the Tarralong Kennels.

male puppies for testicles if you want a stud dog or a show dog. It is difficult to determine this at an early age, but be sure to mention it to the veterinarian for his opinion.

THE PLANNED PARENTHOOD BEHIND YOUR PUPPY

Never be afraid to ask questions about the puppy. Ask to see the mother, and the father if he is on the premises. Ask what they have been fed and what kind of serum they have had so far. Ask if the puppy has been wormed. Many puppies have worms at this age, but your veterinarian should check to see how serious any infection might be and if there has been any damage to the health of the puppy from a heavy infestation. While veterinarians do not always pretend to be experts on every breed, they can point out structural faults or organic problems that should be called to your attention.

PUPPIES AND WORMS

Generally speaking, most puppies—even those raised in clean quarters—come into contact with worms early in life. The worms can be passed down from the mother before birth or picked up during the puppies' first encounters with the ground or their kennel facilities. To say that you must not buy a puppy because of an infestation of worms would be foolish. You might be passing up a fine animal that can be freed of worms in no time with proper treatment and dosage. Let the veterinarian tell you if the worms are too severe or whether the health of the puppy has been endangered.

Let him prescribe the medication, and take the dog for periodic check-ups in the future to keep him free of worms once you have gotten rid of them.

BUYING A SHOW PUPPY

If you wish to buy a show puppy tell the breeder this so they can see that you get a potential show puppy. And if you say you will show it be sure that you mean it. . . it is unfair to take a show quality dog and leave it home on the couch! There are many puppies that have great quality that would suit your needs without being the "best," that the breeder counted on for show wins.

THE PURCHASE PRICE

Pug puppy prices vary according to the breeder's opinion of their potential. There is a pet price and a show potential price. Breeders all usually keep up with the "current" prices and usually charge about the same for their puppies. If you have visited several kennels you will learn this and can decide how much you are willing to pay. Puppies sired by top show dogs naturally come higher and if you want a show dog you must be expected to pay.

A breeder cannot positively promise you a show winner or future champion "at any price" but they should know their own stock and if they have come highly recommended you should be inclined to take their advice on the best puppy for your desires.

Famed dog photographer Joan Ludwig selects this darling picture of Hazel Marten's Pug as one of her favorite puppy pictures.

One of the cutest Pug pictures ever! This little high-stepping black is Mi-Mi's Pearl Bailey, pictured at the age of six weeks. Owned by Mimi Keller, Dallas, Texas.

Breeders usually stand behind their puppies should any congenital defect develop and usually will honor any obligation connected with the original sale.

Be sure to request a diet for the puppy, a copy of the pedigree with registration papers to follow, the privilege of the 24-hour veterinary check-up, and perhaps a favorite toy which will help the puppy make an adjustment to its new home.

THE FIRST NIGHT IN THE NEW HOME

If you are lucky, the new puppy will be so happy and well fed that the first night away from his mother and littermates will be reasonably uneventful. But usually the puppy will miss the companionship and the warmth of his littermates and will cry. Holding the puppy and giving it a food treat along with its favorite toy should help. Leaving the light on or a radio playing should also help. Putting a newspaper-lined box near your bed so you can reassure the puppy (without having to get up!) is easier than running to the kitchen to offer consolation. But there is no easy way to get through that first night! Make the best of it, and the puppy will love you all the more for it!

Also, keep the telephone number of both the breeder and your veterinarian by the phone in case of an emergency or should you have any questions.

Ch. Moran's Masked Marvel, owned by Mr. and Mrs. James Moran of Portland, Oregon. This Group-winning Pug had six Group Placements during 1976, making him a top-winner in the breed for that year.

Chapter 7
Grooming Your Pug

DAILY COAT CARE

Even though your Pug looks well groomed in his natural state, a daily going over with your fingertips to loosen dead hair and to stimulate the skin is a great aid in keeping him looking his best. Follow with a brushing with a soft bristle brush, first going against the lay of the coat and then with it.

BATHING THE PUG

You will be happy to learn that the Pug requires little or no bathing, depending on his life style. If kept clean the pet Pug need never be bathed. The show Pug is something else again. Bathing a few days before the show is sometimes necessary.

Protect the ears with cotton inserts and the eyes with a drop of castor oil. Use lukewarm water, two soapings with a specific Pug dog shampoo, and rinse *thoroughly.* Any soap residue left in the coat will itch and cause the dog to scratch, and will also prevent the natural body oils from coming back into the coat. Then use a creme rinse.

Dry as thoroughly as possible with a turkish towel and put the finishing touches on with a good brushing and a hand dryer.

GROOMING THE SHOW DOG

For each exhibitor there is very likely to be a "perfect" way to prepare a show Pug for the ring. Your best bet is to question the person you bought your dog from on her successful, proven methods of getting her dogs to look good, since the show Pug usually requires trimming.

TRIMMING THE PUG

Trimming is an art and is done with trimming shears. Therefore, it should be taught and observed before trying it yourself. Watch how the exhibitors do it in the grooming areas at the dog shows, or ask to be taught. Areas around the head, tail, rear end and back legs can be cleaned up nicely when you learn how. Choose the best possible teacher for the best possible results.

Trimming should be done as close to the day of the show as possible. In addition to the whiskers and eyebrows it is necessary to trim the hairline that starts at the base of the ear and runs down the neck. Also trim down the swirl on the chest, the hair line down the sides of the tail and the tip of the tail. Certain swirls near the tail and the "pants" should also be trimmed and blended in.

But *NEVER* before learning how to do it from an experienced Pug owner! Always remember, a badly groomed Pug looks a lot worse than one in its natural condition. Practice months before your first show or let a professional do it for you!

After you have trimmed, brush out all the cut hair, apply a drop of Eye Bright to clear the eyes, give a last minute spray of show coat conditioner and finish off.

CHECK LIST FOR GROOMING EQUIPMENT
You will need:
    A pair of rounded end scissors
    A pair of thinning shears for trimming
    A coat conditioner for putting on the final shine
    Small bottle of Eye Bright for clearing the eyes
    A cream conditioner for rubbing in the palms of your hands
        for final highlights
    Petroleum jelly
    Bristle brush
    Cotton swabs

CARE OF THE EARS
Toy breeds that travel close to the ground are frequently in need of having their ears cleaned. At least once each week check to see that the ears are clean and the insides not red from scratching at any foreign matter that might have collected in them.

If they have gotten dirty or wax has collected in them, wipe them out with cotton swabs slightly moistened with baby oil. If the wax accumulation requires removal, try first putting a drop of hydrogen peroxide into the ear and then gently massaging the outside of the ear at the base to help work it out. Leave the peroxide

Pug Puppy Ears

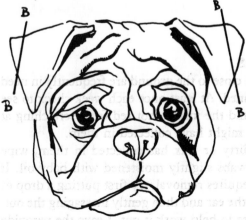

STEP 1.

Open the ear flat and apply adhesive to outside edge of ear only, between arrows—along dotted line.

To assure that your mature Pug has a good ear set, it is recommended that when he begins to cut his second teeth and his ears start to "fly" (fall back into a "rose" position) his ears be kept glued in the correct position. This will train his muscles to hold the ear correctly. The method described here is a simple, painless way to train the puppy's ear muscles. The adhesive is the cement used to apply false eyelashes. We use this because it is less apt to irritate the skin and is easily removed.

STEP 2.

Fold ear along line marked "A"

STEP 3.

Press ear together along line marked "B" and hold between thumb and index finger until glue is set. (Approximately 3 to 5 minutes.)

The puppy's ears should be kept glued until he is completely over his teething period. (Approximately 3 to 8 weeks.)

Mrs. D. E. El-bourn's Caprice of Bournle. The sire was English Ch. Justatwerp of Cedarwood ex English Ch. Genevieve of Bournle. The Bournle Pugs are located in Hampshire, England.

in the ear approximately 15 minutes and then try removing it with the cotton swabs.

If there is any rash or redness, Panalog, obtainable from your veterinarian, will soothe it. If there is continued scratching or rubbing of the ears by the dog, there is the possibility of infection, foreign matter, or ear mites. This requires a visit to the veterinarian.

TOE NAILS

All dogs are extremely sensitive to having their nails cut. A dog is largely dependent upon its feet for its survival, i.e., escaping predators, chasing its food, etc., and this fear of anything endangering their feet stays with them no matter how domesticated they become.

Many dogs wear down their own nails and never need to have their owners trim them. Other dogs require a weekly check to make sure they stay as short as they should be to insure good feet. A simple guide is to see that when the dog is standing in a natural position that none of the nails touch the floor.

If the nails are allowed to grow too long the dog will eventually go down in the pasterns as well as presenting a danger to the eyes when the dog scratches its face.

There are several types of scissors for cutting the nails, or they can be filed. In any case, be sure you hold the dog securely, and have a bright light behind the dogs nail so the "quick" is visible and you do not cut into it. Bleeding is excessive if you do, and usually requires pressure with a swab, a coating of petroleum jelly, or being 'touched' with a styptic pencil to be controlled.

A filing is the safest and quietest method and avoids any accidents with the scissors. It should be done in the same manner as you would file your own nails. If nails are cared for on a regular basis they seldom if ever become too long to cause an actual cutting.

The best way to learn the technique of caring for your dog's nails is to have your veterinarian teach you, or the breeder of your puppy who should have cut the puppy's nails at least once before selling it to you!

For show dogs, a little vaseline rubbed on the black nails will shine them up nicely for their appearance in the ring!

PUG WHISKERS AND EYEBROWS

Those of us that truly love the Pug in its natural form, adore the wonderful black spidery whiskers and eyebrows that grow by the time they mature. If your Pug is to be a pet you may leave them on or cut them off as you prefer. However, if your Pug is to be a show dog they must come off.

Using blunt, or rounded scissors, facing away from the face, trim them off at the base. Be sure you hold the dog securely so there are no accidents with the scissors, and take your time. The hairs that grow out of the moles on the sides of the face should also be removed as well as the long hairs above the eyes. This should be done as close to the day of the show as possible to prevent stubble from marring the dog's appearance, but not at the show where there are too many distractions for an inexperienced dog to cope with in addition to the steel blades so close to his eyes.

THE PUG TRACE

At birth the trace down a Pug's back can be seen as a pencil line

The English
bitch Pegal
Sweet Talk,
owned by Mrs.
S.E. Clements
of Essex,
England.

from the shoulder blades to the base of the tail. When grown the trace represents a wider line of black tipped hairs that present the color pattern known as the trace.

Under normal circumstances the trace is groomed in the same manner as the rest of the body coat. However, for the show dog greater attention can be brought to the presence of a trace—since not all Pugs have one, only those with excellent pigmentation and coloring—by lightly coating your fingers with vaseline and running it along the hairs and blending it in and smoothing it off.

Be careful not to put too much vaseline on to give the dog a "greased line" look, but the touch of vaseline will accent this most admirable and desirable feature.

SHEDDING

All dogs shed, yet the question of just how much is always asked by anyone thinking seriously about buying a dog, especially if the breed is a new one to them.

The Pug dog generally sheds twice a year, spring and fall. Excess hair can be taken care of by daily brushing with a bristle brush during this time and finishing off by "drying your hands" on the coat. Literally, rubbing your hands dry by wiping them off all over the coat. This is a practice done with Siamese cats also!

Fortunately for our breed, they never seem to shed to the point that they cannot be exhibited in the show ring all year round.

Chapter 8
Genetics

No one can guarantee the workings of nature. But, with facts and theories as guides, you can plan, at least on paper, a litter of puppies that should fulfill your fondest expectations. Since the ultimate purpose of breeding is to try to improve the breed, or maintain it at the highest possible standard, such planning should be earnestly undertaken, no matter how uncertain particular elements may be.

There are a few terms with which you should become familiar to help you understand the breeding procedure and the workings of genetics. The first thing that comes to mind is a set of formulae known as the Mendelian Laws. Gregor Mendel was an Austrian cleric and botanist born July 22, 1822 in what is now named Jyncice and is in Czechoslovakia. He developed his theories on heredity by working for several years with garden peas. A paper on his work was published in a scientific journal in 1866, but for many years it went unnoticed. Today the laws derived from these experiments are basic to all studies of genetics and are employed by horticulturists and animal breeders.

To apply these laws to the breeding of dogs, it is necessary to understand the physical aspects of reproduction. First, dogs possess reproductive glands called gonads. The male gonads are the testicles where the sperm (spermatozoa) that impregnate the female are produced. Eggs (ova) are produced in the female gonads (ovaries). When whelped, the bitch possesses in rudimentary form all the eggs that will develop throughout her life, whereas spermatozoa are in continual production within the male gonads. When a bitch is mature enough to reproduce, she periodically comes in heat (estrus). Then a number of eggs descend from the ovaries via the fallopian tubes and enter the two horns of the uterus. There they are fertilized by male sperm deposited in the semen while mating, or they pass out if not fertilized.

In the mating of dogs, there is what is referred to as a tie, a

Australian Champion Westcourt Thor, Best Exhibit in Parade, all Breeds at the 1975 Bairnsdale Show in Australia under Judge Mr. J. R. Ward. Bred by M.G. Downey and owned by Mrs. E. Hall of Victoria, Australia.

period during which anatomical features bind the male and female together and about 600 million spermatozoa are ejected into the female to fertilize the ripened eggs. When a sperm penetrates a ripe egg, zygotes are created and these one-celled future puppies descend from the fallopian tubes, attach themselves to the walls of the uterus, and begin the developmental process of cell production known as mitosis. With all inherited characteristics determined as the zygote was formed, the dam then assumes her role as an incubator for the developing organisms. She has been bred and is in whelp; in these circumstances she also serves in the exchange of gases and in furnishing nourishment for the puppies.

Let us take a closer look at what is happening during the breeding process. We know that the male deposits millions of sperm within the female and that the number of ripe eggs released by the female will determine the number of puppies in the litter. Therefore, those breeders who advertise a stud as a "producer of large litters" do not know the facts or are not sticking to them. The bitch determines the size of the litter; the male sperm determines the sex of the puppies. Half of the millions of sperm involved in a mating carry the characteristic that determines development of a male and the other half carry the factor which triggers development of a female, and distribution of sex is thus decided according to random pairings of sperm and eggs.

Each dog and bitch possesses 39 pairs of chromosomes in each body cell; these pairs are split up in the formation of germ cells so that each one carries half of the hereditary complement. The chromosomes carry the genes, approximately 150,000 like peas in a pod in each chromosome, and these are the actual factors that determine inherited characteristics.

As the chromosomes are split apart and rearranged as to genetic pairings in the production of ova and spermatozoa, every zygote formed by the joining of an egg and a sperm receives 39 chromosomes from each parent. This union will form the pattern of 78 chromosomes inherited from dam and sire, which will be reproduced in every cell of the developing individual, determining what sort of animal it will be.

To understand the procedure more clearly, we must know that there are two kinds of genes—dominant and recessive. A dominant gene is one of a pair whose influence is expressed to the exclusion of the effects of the other. A recessive gene is one of a pair whose influence is subdued by the effects of the other, and characteristics determined by recessive genes become manifest only when both genes of a pairing are recessive. Most of the important qualities we wish to perpetuate in our breeding programs are carried by the dominant genes. It is the successful breeder who becomes expert at eliminating recessive or undesirable genes and building up the dominant or desirable gene patterns.

We have merely touched upon genetics here to point out the importance of planned mating. Any librarian can help you find further information, or books may be purchased offering the very latest findings on canine heredity and genetics. It is a fascinating and rewarding program toward creating better dogs.

111

An excellent portrait of our breed: Ch. Blaylock's Manderin II, owned by Mrs. Rolla Blaylock. The well-wrinkled forehead of this specimen illustrates the characteristic that is one of the breed's hallmarks.

THE POWER IN PEDIGREES

Once you have considered the basics of genetics and realize the strong influence heredity has on your breeding program, you will find yourself compelled to delve into pedigrees of dogs which you may be considering for stud service for your bitches, especially if you intend to breed show dogs.

Someone in the dog fancy once remarked that the definition of a show prospect puppy is one third the pedigree, one third what you see and one third what you *hope* it will be! Well, no matter how you break down your qualifying fractions, we all agree that good breeding is essential if you have any plans at all for a show career for your dog. Many breeders will buy on pedigree alone, counting largely on what they themselves can do with the puppy by way of feeding, conditioning and training. Needless to say, that very important piece of paper commonly referred to as the pedigree is mighty reassuring to a breeder or buyer new at the game, or to one who has a breeding program in mind and is trying to establish his own bloodline.

One of the most fascinating aspects of tracing pedigrees is the way the names of the really great dogs of the past keep appearing in the pedigrees of the great dogs of today—positive proof of the strong influence of heredity and witness to a great deal of truth in the statement that great dogs frequently reproduce themselves, though not necessarily in appearance only. A pedigree represents something of value when one is dedicated to breeding better dogs.

To the novice buyer or one who is perhaps merely switching to another breed and sees only a frolicking, leggy, squirming bundle of energy in a fur coat, a pedigree can mean everything! To those of us who believe in heredity, a pedigree is more like an insurance policy—so always read them carefully and take heed!

For the even more serious breeder of today who wishes to make a further study of bloodlines in relation to his breeding program, the American Kennel Club library stud books can and should be consulted.

113

American and Bermudian Champion Shirrayne's Earthquake Earl takes a Best of Breed rosette at a 1974 show. Handled by Breeder-Owner Shirley Thomas, of the Shirrayne Kennels, Flushing, New York.

Chapter 9
Breeding

Pug dogs have always enjoyed great popularity among dog fanciers and sooner or later the day comes when you ask yourself, "Should I breed her?" Let's assume the time has come for your bitch to be bred and you have decided it would be great fun to have a litter of puppies, and that her puppies would really make a contribution to the breed. The bitch you purchased is sound, her temperament is excellent and she is a most worthy representative of the breed.

There is one essential question you must ask yourself at this point and that is, "Am I prepared to be in constant attendance before, during, and after the arrival of the puppies to insure the safety of the mother and the survival of the puppies?" The structure of the Pug requires constant attention during its whelping and the breeder must be prepared to maintain a constant vigil during this time, OR DON'T BREED! If you are dedicated to the idea of going through this experience with your bitch, then and only then, proceed with your plans to whelp a litter of puppies.

CHOOSING THE STUD

From the moment this idea has crossed your mind you should be thinking about the best possible stud. This involves studying pedigrees, checking out congenital faults, inquiring as to the stud fee, and notifying the owner of the stud of your intentions. When the bitch comes in season notify the owner of the stud immediately and make your appointments for his services.

THE SEASON

As soon as the bitch is actually in season you will notice color, or staining, and a swelling of the vulva. Count off 63 days, and mark the calendar for that date, as well as a full week ahead of schedule since Pugs are notorious early whelpers. While marking the calendar for whelping, count ahead for 10 and 12 days which normally

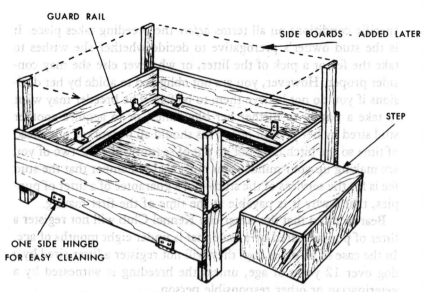

GUARD RAIL

SIDE BOARDS - ADDED LATER

STEP

ONE SIDE HINGED
FOR EASY CLEANING

A representation of a whelping box that can be made by a handy person using items bought in any lumber and hardware shop. The guard rail will prevent the bitch from rolling over onto the pups, and also pressing up against the sides of the box and inadvertently smothering a pup. Several layers of shredded newspapers can be spread about the floor of the box for excellent bedding material, and will be of use in absorbency, too. Each day, the papers should be changed. An old blanket can provide better footing for the newborn pups during their first week.

will be the best time for the actual matings. All bitches, of all breeds, may vary on the best time to be bred, but one indication is that they will usually flag their tails to one side when you scratch their lower back, and will take a firm stand under any pressure from your hands. If you have a male dog in the house they must be separated immediately if he is not to be the sire, since he will express special interest in getting to her at this time.

THE DAY OF THE MATING

The owner of the stud will also be able to tell by the behavior of her stud whether or not the bitch is ready, and if the usual 10 to 12 days is not right for her, you will just have to figure out when it will be. The stud will not be interested if it is not the correct time.

You are entitled to two breedings with ties for the fee, payable at the time of the stud service. Contracts should be written up with specific conditions on all terms *before* the breeding takes place. It is the stud owner's prerogative to decide whether she wishes to take the fee or a pick of the litter, or whatever else she may consider proper. However, you are not obligated to abide by her decisions if you do not believe them to be fair. The breeder may want to take a puppy to further her bloodlines, or to acquire another stud sired by her present one. This should all be worked out ahead of time so the bitch does not go out of season while the two of you are making up your minds! You must also remember that the stud fee is for the services of the stud—not a guarantee of a litter of puppies, that's why it is payable at the time of the first mating.

Bear in mind that the American Kennel Club will not register a litter of puppies sired by a male that is under eight months of age. In the case of an older dog, they will not register a litter sired by a dog over 12 years of age, unless the breeding is witnessed by a veterinarian or other responsible person.

THE COST OF THE STUD FEE

Always try to accompany your bitch for the mating. The disadvantages of sending a bitch away to be bred are numerous. She might not be herself in a strange place, and may be difficult to handle. Air travel or a long car trip may seem a traumatic experience, and some bitches go out of season from the experience of long traveling and handling by strangers.

The stud fee will vary considerably—the better the bloodlines, the more winning the dog does at shows, the higher the fee. You might call other kennels in your area to determine an average, but the best dogs command top fees for their services. However, you will find that they also produce better puppies that bring higher prices!

THE ACTUAL MATING

The owner of the stud will usually help decide which is the best way to bring off a proper breeding. They are familiar with the way their stud performs best and will usually require that you hold your bitch so that she will be calmed by your hands and comforting words.

If the male will not mount on his own initiative, it may be

117

necessary for the owner to assist in lifting him onto the bitch, perhaps even in guiding him to the proper place. Once tied, he may become bored and try to break away. It may be necessary to hold both dogs in place until the tie is broken. Some bitches carry on physically, and vocally, during the tie, but she cannot be hurt in any way so concentration must be given to the stud for a properly executed service.

Many people believe that breeding dogs is simply a matter of placing two dogs, a male and a female, in close proximity, and letting nature take its course. While often this is true, you cannot count on it. Sometimes breeding is hard work and in the case of valuable stock it is essential to supervise, especially if one or both of the dogs are inexperienced. If the owners are also inexperienced it may not take place at all! If this is the case, it's off to the veterinarian!

Care must be taken during the breeding to see that the dogs do not exhaust themselves. In their excitement they can sometimes get "carried away" and overheat themselves to the point of exhaustion. Breed in a cool secluded place without distractions of other people or other dogs, give them a rest every now and then. Never breed on a full stomach, or in the direct sun, or during the hottest part of the day. Small amounts of water when panting excessively can be offered during a rest period.

After the breeding has taken place both should rest, and the bitch should be placed in a crate or carrier and not allowed to run around. If traveling, be sure she rests and has a drink of water before you start off again. This is also a good time for the owners to have a drink!

ARTIFICIAL INSEMINATION

Breeding by means of artificial insemination is usually unsuccessful, unless under a veterinarian's supervision, and can lead to an infection for the bitch and discomfort for the dog if not done exactly correct! Dr. Stephen W.J. Seager, M.V.B., an instructor at the University of Oregon Medical School announced in 1970 that he had been able to preserve dog semen and to produce litters with the stored semen, but it is still very risky, though definitely a possibility for the future, as it is successful now in cattle breeding.

As it stands today, the technique for artificial insemination requires the depositing of semen (taken directly from the dog) into the bitch's vagina, past the cervix and into the uterus by syringe. The correct temperature of the semen, etc., are all vital points necessary to guarantee success, and the procedure is not for inexperienced hands.

THE GESTATION PERIOD

Once the breeding has taken place the seemingly endless waiting period of approximately 63 days begins. For the first ten days after the breeding, you need do absolutely nothing for the bitch. Around the tenth day it is time to begin supplementing the diet with vitamins and calcium. I strongly recommend that you take her to your veterinarian for a list of the proper or perhaps necessary supplements and the correct amounts of each for her particular requirements. Guesses on your part, which may lead to excesses or insufficiencies, can ruin a litter.

The bitch should be free of worms, of course, and if there is any doubt, have the stool checked for them. Your veterinarian will advise you on the necessity and the proper dosage. But never worm a

A mixed bunch . . . . a basketful of Pugs and cats owned by Nancy Gifford, Martlesham Kennels in Suffolk, England.

119

Perpetual Whelping Chart

Bred—Jan. 1 2 3 4 5 6 7 8 9 10 11 12 13 14 15 16 17 18 19 20 21 22 23 24 25 26 27 28 29 30 31
Due—March 5 6 7 8 9 10 11 12 13 14 15 16 17 18 19 20 21 22 23 24 25 26 27 28 29 30 31 **April** 1 2 3 4

Bred—Feb. 1 2 3 4 5 6 7 8 9 10 11 12 13 14 15 16 17 18 19 20 21 22 23 24 25 26 27 28
Due—April 5 6 7 8 9 10 11 12 13 14 15 16 17 18 19 20 21 22 23 24 25 26 27 28 29 30 **May** 1 2

Bred—Mar. 1 2 3 4 5 6 7 8 9 10 11 12 13 14 15 16 17 18 19 20 21 22 23 24 25 26 27 28 29 30 31
Due—May 3 4 5 6 7 8 9 10 11 12 13 14 15 16 17 18 19 20 21 22 23 24 25 26 27 28 29 30 31 **June** 1 2

Bred—Apr. 1 2 3 4 5 6 7 8 9 10 11 12 13 14 15 16 17 18 19 20 21 22 23 24 25 26 27 28 29 30
Due—June 3 4 5 6 7 8 9 10 11 12 13 14 15 16 17 18 19 20 21 22 23 24 25 26 27 28 29 30 **July** 1 2

Bred—May 1 2 3 4 5 6 7 8 9 10 11 12 13 14 15 16 17 18 19 20 21 22 23 24 25 26 27 28 29 30 31
Due—July 3 4 5 6 7 8 9 10 11 12 13 14 15 16 17 18 19 20 21 22 23 24 25 26 27 28 29 30 31 **August** 1 2

Bred—June 1 2 3 4 5 6 7 8 9 10 11 12 13 14 15 16 17 18 19 20 21 22 23 24 25 26 27 28 29 30
Due—August 3 4 5 6 7 8 9 10 11 12 13 14 15 16 17 18 19 20 21 22 23 24 25 26 27 28 29 30 31 **Sept.** 1

Bred—July 1 2 3 4 5 6 7 8 9 10 11 12 13 14 15 16 17 18 19 20 21 22 23 24 25 26 27 28 29 30 31
Due—September 2 3 4 5 6 7 8 9 10 11 12 13 14 15 16 17 18 19 20 21 22 23 24 25 26 27 28 29 30 **Oct.** 1 2

Bred—Aug. 1 2 3 4 5 6 7 8 9 10 11 12 13 14 15 16 17 18 19 20 21 22 23 24 25 26 27 28 29 30 31
Due—October 3 4 5 6 7 8 9 10 11 12 13 14 15 16 17 18 19 20 21 22 23 24 25 26 27 28 29 30 31 **Nov.** 1 2

Bred—Sept. 1 2 3 4 5 6 7 8 9 10 11 12 13 14 15 16 17 18 19 20 21 22 23 24 25 26 27 28 29 30
Due—November 3 4 5 6 7 8 9 10 11 12 13 14 15 16 17 18 19 20 21 22 23 24 25 26 27 28 29 30 **Dec.** 1 2

Bred—Oct. 1 2 3 4 5 6 7 8 9 10 11 12 13 14 15 16 17 18 19 20 21 22 23 24 25 26 27 28 29 30 31
Due—December 3 4 5 6 7 8 9 10 11 12 13 14 15 16 17 18 19 20 21 22 23 24 25 26 27 28 29 30 31 **Jan.** 1 2

Bred—Nov. 1 2 3 4 5 6 7 8 9 10 11 12 13 14 15 16 17 18 19 20 21 22 23 24 25 26 27 28 29 30
Due—January 3 4 5 6 7 8 9 10 11 12 13 14 15 16 17 18 19 20 21 22 23 24 25 26 27 28 29 30 31 **Feb.** 1

Bred—Dec. 1 2 3 4 5 6 7 8 9 10 11 12 13 14 15 16 17 18 19 20 21 22 23 24 25 26 27 28 29 30 31
Due—February 2 3 4 5 6 7 8 9 10 11 12 13 14 15 16 17 18 19 20 21 22 23 24 25 26 27 28 **March** 1 2 3 4

pregnant bitch after the third week!

Tell your veterinarian at this time the anticipated arrival date of the puppies so he can mark his calendar, and tell him you will call again to remind him as the "big day" gets closer.

EXERCISING THE BITCH IN WHELP

The pregnant bitch will normally lead her usual life style while awaiting the birth of the puppies. As she approaches the termination of the gestation period you will notice that she slows down from the extra weight she is carrying and will do a great deal more sleeping. However, she must also continue to get sufficient exercise. More walking and less strenuous running or jumping would be advised, though animals usually display a remarkable intuition about what is good and bad for them while they are in whelp. The instinct for motherhood is so strong that the silliest of bitches becomes a sensible brooder when it is required of her.

PROBING FOR PUPPIES

Far too many breeders are overanxious about whether the breeding "took" and are inclined to feel for puppies or try to persuade a veterinarian to radiograph or X-ray their bitches to confirm it. Unless there is reason to doubt the normalcy of a pregnancy, this is risky. Why risk endangering the litter by probing with inexperienced hands? Few bitches give no evidence of being in whelp, and there is no need to prove it by trying to count puppies.

ALERTING YOUR VETERINARIAN

At least a week before the puppies are due, you should notify your veterinarian that you expect the litter and give him the date and full particulars of the pregnancy. Some veterinarians suggest that you call them again when the bitch starts labor so that they may further plan their time, should they be needed. Discuss this matter with him and find out how he feels he can best see that he or an assistant will be available.

LATE ARRIVALS

While most Pug puppies arrive early, you must be especially aware of late arrivals. If your bitch delays any longer than 65 days an immediate visit to the veterinarian is required. The rate of growth in puppies during those last days is tremendous, and the more they grow inside the mother, the harder it is going to be for them to be whelped, especially in this breed where the dogs' heads are large.

Therefore, if you see that the bitch is ready and trying to whelp without success, or that she is overdue, it may be a question of life and death for both her and the puppies if you do not seek the advice of your veterinarian on the proper care.

DO YOU NEED A VETERINARIAN IN ATTENDANCE?

Most animal births are accomplished without complications, and you should call for veterinary assistance only if you run into trouble.

Your bitch will appreciate as little interference and as few strangers around as possible. A quiet place, with her nest, a single

Pugs used in breeding programs must be of excellent "type." One such fine specimen is English Ch. Paramin Polanaise of Hoonme, owned by Mrs. A. Williams, Hoonme Pugs, Wilts, England. She was the 1975 Crufts champion and Best of Breed winner.

familiar face and her own instincts are all that is necessary for nature to take its course. An audience of curious children squealing and questioning, other pets nosing around, or strange adults should be avoided. Many a bitch which has been distracted in this way has been known to devour her young. There are other ways of teaching children the miracle of birth, and the bitch is entitled to her privacy.

LABOR

Many Pug litters—especially first litters—do not run the full term of 63 days, and may come as much as a week early! So a full week ahead of their anticipated arrival it is time to start making your vigil! You must begin to observe the bitch for signs of the commencement of labor. This will manifest itself in the form of ripples running down the sides of her body, which will come as a revelation to her as well. It is most noticeable when she is lying on her side—and she will be sleeping a great deal as the arrival date comes closer. If she is sitting or walking about, she will perhaps sit down quickly or squat peculiarly. As the ripples become more frequent, birth time is drawing near. Do not leave her! Usually within 24 hours before whelping, she will stop eating, and as much as a week before she will begin digging a nest. The bitch should be given something resembling a whelping box with layers of newspaper (black and white print only) to make her nest. She will dig more and more as birth approaches. This is the time to make your promise to stop interfering unless your help is specifically required. Some bitches whimper and others are silent, but whimpering does not necessarily indicate trouble so—stay cool!

THE ARRIVAL OF THE PUPPIES

The sudden gush of green fluid from the bitch indicates that the water or fluid surrounding the puppies has "broken" and they are about to start down the canal and come into the world. When the water breaks, birth of the first puppy is imminent. The first puppies are usually born within minutes to a half hour of each other, but a couple of hours between the later ones is not uncommon. If you notice the bitch straining constantly without producing a puppy, or if a puppy remains partially in and partially out for too long, it is cause for concern. Breech births (puppies born feet first instead of head first) can often cause delay and are often a problem which requires veterinary assistance.

Pugs and most other breeds with uneven bites are often unable to bite the cords easily or quickly enough to free the puppy from the sac. It will be necessary for you to be present to do this for her so that the puppy does not drown or get injured in her frantic attempt to scratch off the sac with her feet. Also Pugs that carry too much weight are often unable to get their heads around to their rear end to deliver a difficult puppy and your assistance will again be necessary. These are just two more reasons for you to be sure you are present when she whelps.

FEEDING THE BITCH BETWEEN BIRTHS

Usually the bitch will not be interested in food for about 24 hours before the arrival of the puppies, and perhaps as long as two or three days after their arrival. The placenta which she devours after each puppy is high in food value and will be more than ample to sustain her. This is nature's way of allowing the mother to feed herself and her babies without having to leave the nest and hunt for food during the first crucial days. The mother always cleans up all traces of birth in the wilds so as not to attract other animals to her newborn babies.

However, there are those of us who believe in making food available should the mother feel the need to restore or maintain her strength during or after delivery. Raw chopped meat, beef bouillon, and milk are all acceptable and may be offered to her and placed near the whelping box during the first two or three days. After that, the mother will begin to put the babies on a sort of schedule. She will leave the whelping box at frequent intervals, take longer exercise periods, and begin to take interest in other things. This is where the fun begins for you. Now the babies are no longer soggy little pinkish blobs. They begin to crawl around and squeal and hum and grow before your very eyes!

It is at this time, if all has gone normally, that the family can be introduced gradually and great praise and affection given to the mother for a job well done!

BREECH BIRTHS

Puppies normally are delivered head first. However, some are

Above: Ch. Oliver Twist and four of six puppies from a litter he sired out of Ch. Gayberry Victoria of Gore. Owner Romola L. Hicks, Chapel Hill, North Carolina. **Below:** Pelshire's Wisselwood Magic, co-owned by Susan B. Burnham and Doris Aldrich of Cheshire, Connecticut.

Ch. Wolf's Kauffee Royal Rose, C.D. pictured here at three months of age. Bred and owned by Esther Wolf of Omaha, Nebraska.

presented feet first, or in other abnormal positions, and this is referred to as a "breech birth." Assistance is often necessary to get the puppy out of the birth canal. Great care must be taken not to injure the puppy or the dam.

Aid can be given by grasping the puppy with a piece of turkish toweling and pulling gently during the dam's contractions. Be careful not to squeeze the puppy too hard; merely try to ease it out by moving it gently back and forth and out. Because even this much delay in delivery may mean the puppy is drowning, do not wait for the bitch to remove the sac. Do it yourself by tearing the sac open to expose the face and head. Then cut the cord with sterile scissors anywhere from one-half to three-quarters of an inch away from the navel. If the cord bleeds excessively, pinch the end of it with your fingers and count five. Repeat if necessary. Then pry open the mouth with your finger and hold the puppy upside down for a moment to drain any fluids from the lungs. Next, rub the puppy briskly with turkish or paper toweling. You should get it wriggling and whimpering by this time.

It is best to allow the bitch to take care of at least the first puppy all by herself to preserve the natural instinct and to provide the nutritive values obtained by her consumption of the afterbirths.

DRY BIRTHS

Occasionally the sac will break before the delivery of a puppy and will be expelled while the puppy remains inside, thereby depriving the dam of the necessary lubrication to expel the puppy normally. Inserting a thin coating of vaseline or mineral oil via your finger will help the puppy pass down the birth canal. This emergency is yet another reason for you to be present during the whelping so that you can count the puppies and afterbirths to be sure none are retained by the mother.

THE TWENTY FOUR HOUR CHECKUP

It is smart to have a veterinarian check the mother and her puppies within 24 hours after the last puppy is born. The veterinarian can check for cleft palates or umbilical hernia and may wish to give the dam—particularly if she is a show dog—an injection of Pituitin to make sure of the expulsion of all afterbirths and to tighten up the uterus. This can prevent a sagging belly after the puppies are weaned and the bitch is being readied for the show ring once again.

FALSE PREGNANCY

The disappointment of a false pregnancy is almost as bad for the owner as it is for the bitch. She goes through the gestation period with all the symptoms—swollen stomach, increased appetite, swollen bright pink nipples—even makes a nest when the time comes. You may even take an oath that you noticed the nipples on her body from the labor pains. Then, just as suddenly as you made up your mind that she was definitely going to have puppies, you will know that she definitely is not! She may walk around carrying a toy as if it were a puppy for a few days, but she will soon be back to normal and acting just as if nothing happened—and nothing did!

Phay's Dixie Hypotheses, C.D.X. and his owner Glen Wells of Little Rock, Arkansas. "Chester" was her first obedience Pug and is pictured here with the ribbons and trophies won as the Highest Scoring Dog in Trial at the 1964 Little Rock Dog Training Club event.

CAESAREAN SECTION

Should the whelping reach the point where there is a complication, such as the bitch's not being capable of whelping the puppies herself, the "moment of truth" is upon you and a Caesarean section may be necessary. The bitch may be too small or too immature to expel the puppies herself; or her cervix may fail to dilate enough to allow the young to come down the birth canal; or there may be torsion of the uterus, a dead or monster puppy, a sideways puppy blocking the canal, or perhaps toxemia. A Caesarean section will be the only solution. No matter what the cause, get the bitch to the veterinarian immediately to insure your chances of saving the mother and the puppies.

The Caesarean section operation (the name derived from the idea that Julius Caesar was delivered by this method) involves the removal of the unborn young from the uterus of the dam by surgical incision into the walls through the abdomen. The operation is performed when it has been determined that for some reason the puppies cannot be delivered normally. While modern surgical methods have made the operation itself reasonably safe, with the dam being perfectly capable of nursing the puppies shortly after the completion of the surgery, the chief danger lies in the ability to spark life into the puppies immediately upon their removal from the womb, and the ability of the mother to cope with the anesthesia. If the mother dies, the time element is even more important in saving the young, since the oxygen supply ceases upon the death of the dam, and the difference between life and death is measured in seconds.

After surgery, when the bitch is home in her whelping box with the babies, she will probably nurse the young without distress. You must be sure that the sutures are kept clean and that no redness or swelling or ooze appears in the wound. Healing will take place naturally, and no salves or ointments should be applied unless prescribed by the veterinarian, for fear the puppies will get

Overleaf: Original oil painting by famous Spanish painter Francisco Ubeda Marin, featuring three of Tracy Williams' Pugs. **L. to R.:** Am., Brazilian Ch. Shirrayne's Golddigger, Brazilian Ch. Fischer's Nitty Gritty and Brazilian Ch. Shirrayne's Jungle Jim.

Am. Can. Cuban and Bermudian Ch. Pugville's Mighty Jim with a litter of his puppies whelped in June, 1954 at Mrs. Filomena Doherty's Pugville Kennels in Washington Crossing, Pennsylvania. The puppy in the center was Pugville's Sunshine Nelly, owned by singer Lena Horne.

it into their systems. If there is any doubt, check the bitch for fever, restlessness (other than normal concern for her young) or a lack of appetite, but do not anticipate trouble.

DANGER SIGNALS

While you have had your bitch examined for perfect health *before* she is bred, and there is no reason to anticipate trouble in a breeding, there are certain danger signals you will notice should there be an emergency.

Any indication of fever, lack of appetite, change in behavior pattern, diarrhea, discharge, tenderness anywhere on the body, sit-

Perhaps the most famous of all paintings which include a Pug dog is this William Hogarth oil on canvas, entitled The Painter and his Pug, rendered in 1745. The original 35½ x 27½ painting hangs in the Tate Gallery, London.

Right: Lovely portrait of Donaldson's Tigger and Donaldson's Sissy, bred by Wayne and Marie Donaldson. **Below:** Ivanwold Gayberry Troubador winning a major on the way to championship under Irene Khatoonian Schlintz, just 10 days after turning six months old. Tuffy is co-owned by Mrs. Romola L. Hicks and Dr. and Mrs. Edward Patterson, Ivanwold Kennels. He is shown by Dr. Patterson.

ting in corners, throwing up, whimpering or crying, or inability to sleep mean a trip to the veterinarian!

DANGER SIGNALS FROM NEWBORN PUPPIES

Puppies must be watched carefully no matter how much the mother is pleased with herself and her newborn litter. Healthy puppies have a "healthy cry" and you will recognize the cry of a sick puppy if you have ever heard one! They might also smell sour, have diarrhea, swollen stomachs, uneven breathing, not eat, and in the case of most all puppies, of all breeds, if they sleep on their backs or are found off in a corner of the whelping box by themselves.

Nature provides the dam with the instinct to recognize an unhealthy puppy and she will usually push it off to the side or bury it under the papers in a corner rather than try to feed it. Once this happens you either feed it and try to keep it alive yourself, or you allow nature to take its course. It is usually wiser to let nature take its course, since puppies brought up after rejection by the mother are usually sickly all their lives or break your heart when they eventually die as the dam knew from the beginning.

There are several things that can strike the mother and her young during this period that are best diagnosed by your veterinarian, but the symptoms mentioned here are your clue for help to save them.

SOCIALIZING YOUR PUPPY

The need for puppies to get out among other animals and people cannot be stressed enough. Kennel-reared dogs are subject to all sorts of idiosyncrasies and seldom make good house dogs or are able to adapt to the world around them after they have left the kennel.

The crucial age, which determines the personality and general behavior patterns that will predominate during the rest of the dog's life, comes between the ages of three and ten weeks. This is particularly true during the 21st and 28th day. It is essential that the puppy be socialized during this time by bringing him into the family life as much as possible. Floor surfaces, indoor and outdoors, should be experienced; handling by all members of the family and visitors is important; preliminary grooming gets him used to a lifelong necessity; light training, such as setting him up

134

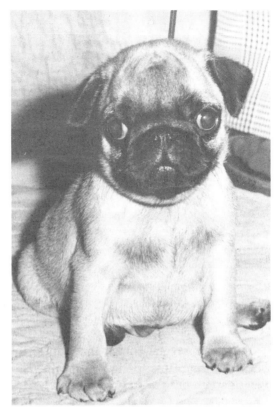

Another of Mimi Keller's typy Pug puppies ... This eight-week-old fawn is Mi-Mi's Mr. Phurst Double Copy.

on tables and cleaning teeth and ears and cutting nails, etc., has to be started early if he is to become a show dog. The puppy should be exposed to car riding, shopping tours, a leash around its neck, children, his name, etc., in order for him to develop relationships with humans.

It is up to the breeder, of course, to protect the puppy from harm or injury during this initiation into the outside world. The benefits reaped from proper attention will pay off in the long run with a well-behaved, well-adjusted grown dog capable of becoming an integral part of a happy family.

Overleaf: Ch. Jo Nol's Holiday Harmony pictured winning Best of Breed at the 1975 Kennel Club of Beverly Hills show under Merrill Cohen. Handled by Daisy Austed for owner Joan L. Nolan of Reseda, California.

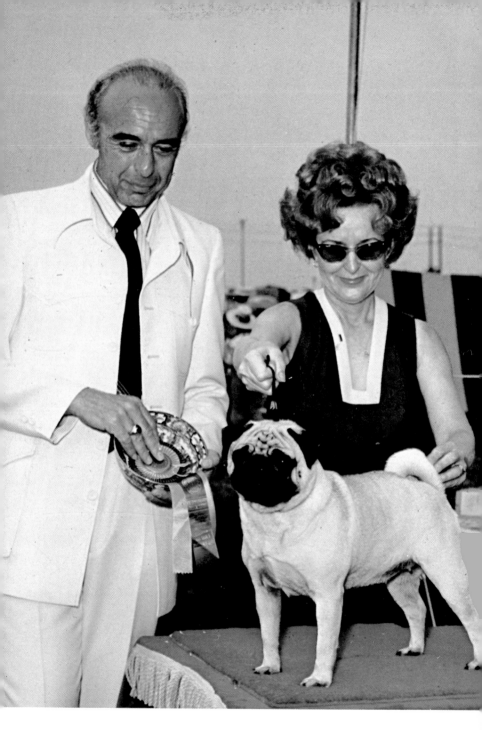

BEST OF
WINNERS

ASHBEY PHOTO

Donger's Princess Valentine with her first litter of puppies, four of which became champions. "Cindy" was named Outstanding Producer for 1971 according to *Kennel Review* magazine, and her second litter produced three champions. Co-owned by Donald Foral and Roger Perry, Donger's Kennel, Indianapolis.

Overleaf, top: An early start on a show career . . . three-month-old Rao's Duchess of Hyderabad wins Best in Match over an entry of 300 puppies at a 1975 show under judge Carroll Overby. Owned by Dr. and Mrs. A.M. Rao and handled for them by Paul R. Jolley. **Bottom:** Ch. Sabbaday Titus, bred by Sabbaday Kennels and co-owned with Polly J. Lamarine, Silvertown Pugs, Meriden, Conn. The sire was Sabbaday Sabateur ex Sabbaday Fantasy.

Chapter 10
Feeding and Nutrition

FEEDING PUPPIES

There are many diets today for young puppies, including all sorts of products on the market for feeding the newborn, for supplementing the feeding of the young and for adding this or that to diets depending on what is lacking in the way of a complete diet.

When weaning puppies, it is necessary to put them on four meals a day, even while you are tapering off with the mother's milk. Feeding at six in the morning, noontime, six in the evening and midnight is about the best schedule, since it fits in with most human eating plans. Meals for the puppies can be prepared immediately before or after your own meals, without too much of a change in your own schedule.

6 A.M.

Two meat and two milk meals serve best and should be served alternately, of course. Assuming the 6 A.M. feeding is a milk meal, the contents should be as follows: Goat's milk is the very best milk to feed puppies but is expensive and usually available only at drug stores unless you live in farm country. This meal should contain evaporated milk (later powdered milk) diluted two parts milk and one part water, along with a raw egg yolk, honey or Karo syrup, sprinkled with high-protein baby cereal and some wheat germ. As the puppies mature, cottage cheese may be added or, at one of the two milk meals, it can be substituted for the cereal. A little Knox gelatin should also be sprinkled on and mixed through, as well as two 5-grain pills of calcium phosphate, powdered, per pint mixture.

Overleaf, top: Ch. Donaldson's Rinestone Cowboy is taking 3-point major under Alfred Treen, 1976 Tulsa Show. Bred, owned, handled by Marie Donaldson. **Bottom:** Ch. Peers Koonie winning under Alice Gretton, 1976 Texas Show. Breeder-owners are Mary and Jack Peer of Dallas; handler is Jack Potts.

NOONTIME

Feed a puppy chow that has been soaked in warm water or beef broth or bouillion, and mixed with raw or simmered chopped meat with a vitamin powder.

6 P.M.

Repeat the milk meal, perhaps varying the type of cereal in the form of shredded wheat soaked, or rice or corn cereal.

MIDNIGHT

Repeat the meat meal. If raw meat was fed at noon, the evening meal might be simmered. Serve all food room temperature or heated until it is warm. Keep left-overs refrigerated.

Please note that specific proportions on this diet are not given. Your veterinarian should advise you on the correct amounts for your puppy, but a good indication is whether the puppy eats it all. If the dish is empty increase the amount very slowly. If food is left, feed a little less until the dish is empty.

The puppies should each "have their fill," because growth is very rapid at this age. If they have not satisfied themselves, increase the amount so that they do not have to fight for the last morsel. They will not overeat if they know there is enough food available. Instinct will usually let them eat to suit their normal capacity.

If there is any doubt in your mind as to any ingredient you are feeding, ask yourself, "Would I give it to my own baby?" If the answer is no, then don't give it to your puppies. At this age, the comparison between puppies and human babies can be a good guide.

If there is any doubt in your mind, I repeat: ask your veterinarian to be sure.

Many puppies will regurgitate their food, perhaps a couple of

Overleaf, top: Winner of the Sweepstakes at the 1977 Specialty Show of the Pug Dog Club of Greater New York was Gloria Camileri's Cambrookes Kojak III. This show, held in conjunction with the Westchester Kennel Club, was judged by Joan Brearley. Kojak was handled for the owner by John Marsh. Al Meshira, club president, presented the trophy. **Bottom:** Ch. Reko's Wee Ping-A-Pug, owned by Paul V. Lipka of La Jolla, California, and pictured winning at a 1976 show under judge Richard Guevara. Handled by Lee Redding.

Ch. Candy's Bit O'Jolly, finished for his championship in three shows and while under eleven months of age, with three five-point majors. Owned by Mrs. Muriel Dusek of Norfolk, Conn.

Stormie and his champion sons, Tempest and Yardi. These Martlesham Pugs are officially Ch. Stormie of Martlesham, Ch. Yardi of Martlesham and Ch. Tempest.

Overleaf, top: 18-month-old Harper's Miss In A Minute wins Best of Winners from Bred-by Exhibitor Class at 1976 Pug Dog Club of Maryland Specialty under Dawn Vick. Handler Alan L. Harper, Jacksonville. **Bottom:** Family affair! Erica Huggins awards Best of Breed to Ch. Donaldson's Goodtime Charlie, owner-handled by Ivan Crowell; Best of Winners to Donaldson's Rinestone Cowboy, with owner-handler Marie Donaldson; and Winners Bitch to Donaldson's Lil Tweety Bird, owner John Brown. Show was 1976 Omaha show.

PUG DOG CLUB
GREATER NEW YORK
FEBRUARY 9, 1975

FIRST PLACE
BRED BY EXHIB.
DOG

BUSHMAN PHOTO

times, before they manage to retain it. If they do bring up their food, allow them to eat it again, rather than clean it away. Sometimes additional saliva is necessary for them to digest it, and you do not want them to skip a meal just because it is an unpleasant sight for you to observe.

This same regurgitation process holds true sometimes with the bitch, who will bring up her own food for her puppies every now and then. This is a natural instinct on her part which stems from the days when dogs gave birth in the wild. The only food the mother could provide at weaning time was too rough and indigestible for her puppies. Therefore, she took it upon herself to pre-digest the food until it could be taken and retained by her young. Bitches today will sometimes resort to this, especially bitches who love having litters and have a strong maternal instinct. Some dams will help you wean their litters and even give up feeding entirely once they see you are taking over.

WEANING THE PUPPIES

When weaning the puppies the mother is kept away from the little ones for longer and longer periods of time. This is done over a period of several days. At first she is separated from the puppies for several hours, then all day, leaving her with them only at night for comfort and warmth. This gradual separation aids in helping the mother's milk to dry up gradually, and she suffers less distress after feeding a litter.

If the mother continues to carry a great deal of milk with no signs of its tapering off, consult your veterinarian before she gets too uncomfortable. She may cut the puppies off from her supply of milk too abruptly if she is uncomfortable, before they should be completely on their own.

Overleaf: Goodwin's Dixie Darling winning Best of Breed at the 1975 Plainview Texas Kennel Club show under Harold Bishop. The sire was Goodwin's Anxious Andy ex Ch. Goodwin's Georgy Girl. Bred, owned and handled by Shirley Goodwin of St. Petersburg, Florida. **Bottom:** Alexander's Sump'tin F'r Nuttin wins the Bred by Exhibitor Class at the 1975 Pug Dog Club of America show under judge Dr. W. Edward McGough. Shown by breeder-owner Joan Alexander of New Orleans, Louisiana.

Lovely head study of Ch. Robertson's Buc-O Nunnally in a wistful moment. Owned by Stony Robertson and Louise V. Gore, Louisville, Kentucky.

There are many opinions on the proper age to start weaning puppies. If you plan to start selling them between six and eight weeks, weaning should begin between two and three weeks of age. Here again, each bitch will pose a different situation. The size and weight of the litter should help determine the time, and your veterinarian will have an opinion, as he determines the burden the bitch is carrying by the size of the litter and her general condition. If she is being pulled down by feeding a large litter, he may suggest that you start at two weeks. If she is glorying in her motherhood without any apparent taxing of her strength, he may suggest three to four weeks. You and he will be the best judges. But remember, there is no substitute that is as perfect as mother's milk—and the longer the puppies benefit from it, the better. Other food yes, but mother's milk first and foremost for the healthiest puppies!

Overleaf, top: Ch. Ken M's Bingo Bengy wins Stud Dog Class at 1975 City of Angels PDC Specialty. Ch. Paulaine's Lightfoot is next, owned-bred by Paul and Elaine Lipka; Paulaine's Tic-A-Long, owned by Shirley and Lee Redding; at right is Ken M's Its A Joy, bred-owned by Ken and Diana Mulhern. **Bottom:** Bonjor's Reluctant Tiger goes Best of Breed at PDCA Specialty under Elizabeth Elbourn. John J. Marsh, Dr. Arthur Reinitz, Susanne Rowe complete picture.

BEST OF
BREED

ASHBEY PHOTO

STATEN ISLAND K.C.
JUNE 25 1972

BEST
OF
WINNERS

BEST OF
OPPOSITE

GILBERT PHOTO

ORPHANED PUPPIES

The ideal solution of feeding orphaned puppies is to be able to put them with another nursing dam who will take them on as her own. If this is not possible within your own kennel, or a kennel that you know of, it is up to you to care for and feed the puppies. Survival is possible but requires a great deal of time and effort on your part.

Your substitute formula must be precisely prepared, always served heated to body temperature and refrigerated when not being used. Esbilac, a vacuum-packed powder, with complete feeding instructions on the can, is excellent and about as close to mother's milk as you can get. If you can't get Esbilac, or until you do get Esbilac, there are two alternative formulas that you might use.

Mix one part boiled water with five parts of evaporated milk and add one teaspoonful of di-calcium phosphate per quart of formula. Di-calcium phosphate can be secured at any drug store. If they have it in tablet form only, you can powder the tablets with the back part of a tablespoon. The other formula for newborn puppies is a combination of eight ounces of homogenized milk mixed well with two egg yolks.

You will need doll bottles or plastic eyedroppers that should contain the formula proportionate to the puppies' size, age and growth. Their stomachs should look full after a feeding, or slightly larger than when you began, but never distended. The feedings should be anywhere from every two hours to every six hours, again depending on age and size. Check with your veterinarian to see that you are using proper amounts and are feeding the puppies properly. At two to three weeks you can start adding Pablum to the formula and beef baby food from your finger as soon as they'll take it. Esbilac can also be mixed in.

It will be necessary to burp the puppy just as you would a human baby, patting and rubbing it gently. This will also encourage the puppy to defecate, which it must do after each meal. If the puppy does not do it on its own, rub its stomach or under its tail gently until it does.

You must also keep the puppies clean. If there is diarrhea or if they bring up a little formula, they should be wiped off with a warm, wet towel and dried off thoroughly.

ADDITIONAL SUPPLEMENTS

Vitamins are a controversial subject with both breeders and owners. Some say that if a puppy is fed properly with the very best quality food, vitamins are unnecessary. Others say that while puppies are growing, they need every possible assistance and vitamins are essential. Therefore, we advise a consultation with your veterinarian to get his opinion on how your puppies are progressing and which vitamins and how much of them you may give.

With the extremely young puppy, cod liver oil or something like it should be added to the formula, especially if you live in a cold climate and have a winter litter.

Some breeders powder a kelp tablet and add to the formula to aid pigmentation.

EATING ON THEIR OWN

The best time to start adding "solids" to the diet during the weaning period varies with your puppies, just as it varies with babies. As far as Pugs are concerned the average time to start adding raw chopped meat and tuna fish is anywhere from three to four weeks. Try a very small amount after three weeks and see how rapidly they take to it. Once they get used to it let them set the amount they want to eat, and let the mother finish up what is left.

While most puppies will eat from your finger, teaspoons or demitasse spoons are good for feeding, and at this transition period and at about this age they should be up to about five to ten

---

Overleaf, top: Ch. Dhandy's English Knickers, Group Winning stud at the Tampa, Fla. kennels of Mr. and Mrs. E.G. Willard. Photo by Al Paul. **Bottom:** First place Blue Ribbon winner at the 1975 Maryland State Fair was Dr. Robert L. Gossweiler's original design hooked rug, worked by him in the image of one of his dogs.

demitasse spoonfuls. They should be perfectly capable of eating on their own at this time and if they are reluctant, you had better take another look at them to see if there is a throat obstruction or cleft palate.

Also, once they are eating on their own, do not suddenly take them from their mother. Taper them off, by only leaving her with them at night, while you take over the feeding schedule in the daytime.

At six weeks of age they should be put on a high quality puppy meal mixed with broth and/or rice with their raw meat, or bits of liver. To give them every benefit, still keep them on the formula for a while until they are accustomed to the kibble, or meal. The mother will let you know when she feels they are completely weaned and will stay away from them when they are hungry. It is usually around six weeks, but some mothers want to take them a little further so let her be the best judge. When the puppies start digging their teeth into her she will soon call a halt to their feeding from her. In the meantime, the puppies have received every possible benefit from her which can only add to their good health.

SALTING THE FOOD
Since Pugs are inclined to pant a great deal because of their short noses, they lose a great deal of sodium from their bodies. Sprinkling their food with salt, very much as you would your own, will help replace this, especially in summer.

SOCIAL ERRORS
Pugs, like other short-nosed breeds, are inclined to "wolf down" their food as well as swallow a great deal of air when they eat. This causes gas in the stomach when they feed. It mixes with the natural gases in the stomach required to digest their food, passes on into their intestines during the process and eventually must find a way out of their bodies.

Overleaf: Future champion Higman's Little Heller, pictured at two months of age with Derek Higman at two weeks of age. Breeder/owners—of both—are Ron and Shari Higman of Miami, Florida.

Two Pug puppies from the kennels of Shirley Thomas, Flushing, New York. Right, Ch. Shirrayne's Victorious Vance, Best of Winners at the 1978 Pug Dog Club of Greater New York Specialty Show and his pal, Shirrayne's Vivacious Verne.

If the gas is particulary offensive there may be a digestive upset indicated, or a change in the brand of kibble or chow that is being fed may be necessary. And be sure that only the best grades of meat be fed, since spoiled meat can be a cause of bad odor. Garlic powder sprinkled through the food will not only sweeten their breath, but aid in digestion and perhaps help as well.

However, the best way to avoid embarrassment is to walk the dog after eating, keep it away from company for a few hours after eating—and to feed only the best foods. It won't prevent gas, but it will help!

DRINKING WATER

Need we say that drinking water, fresh, clean and cool, is *essential* to all dogs, and especially the dogs that pant heavily or have short noses? Water should be available at all times, changed at least twice a day and offered when traveling any distance. If your dog does not drink enough water, salting the food will help. Pugs

Above: Sue Ann Felsen's six month old Pug pup, Shirrayne's Quizzy Quickwit. Sue Ann is a Pug fancier from Brooklyn. **Below:** Ch. Broughcastle Balladeer, owned, handled and bred by Douglas Huffman, is shown wining the Toy Group under Nick Calicura at a recent Lexington Kennel Club show.

Above: An advertising card for the Merrick Thread Company of many years ago. From the collection of Mariann Johnson of Enid, Oklahoma. **Below:** An old Victorian post card featuring a mother Pug and her brood, printed in England and owned by Shirley Thomas.

are neat drinkers so there is no excuse for it not to be there for them at all times.

FEEDING THE BITCH IN WHELP

The bitch in whelp will usually show an increase in appetite as her pregnancy progresses. She will require more food, more often. Instead of the usual one meal a day, feed twice a day, and as time goes by perhaps three times a day, or snacks in between meals. She will let you know her capacity either by licking the dish clean or by walking away and finishing up later.

This is the time when good red meat should be featured in increasing amounts, with the addition of vegetables, eggs, and perhaps fruits to the diet. Your veterinarian will advise you on essentials.

OBESITY

As we mentioned above, there are many "perfect" diets for your dogs on the market today. When fed in proper proportions, they should keep your dogs in full bloom. However, there are those owners who, more often than not, indulge their own appetites and are inclined to overfeed their dogs as well. A study in Great Britain in the early 1970's found that a major percentage of obese people also had obese dogs. The entire family was overfed and all suffered from the same condition.

Obesity in dogs is a direct result of the animal's being fed more food than he can properly "burn up" over a period of time, so it is stored as fat or fatty tissue in the body. Pet dogs are more inclined to become obese than show dogs or working dogs, but obesity is a factor to be considered with the older dog, since his exercise is curtailed.

A lack of "tuck up" on a dog, or not being able to feel the ribs, or great folds of fat which hang from the underside of the dog can all be considered as obesity. Genetic factors may enter into the picture, but usually the owner is at fault.

The life span of the obese dog is decreased on several counts. Excess weight puts undue stress on the heart as well as the joints. The dog becomes a poor anesthetic risk and has less resistance to viral or bacterial infections. Treatment is seldom easy or completely effective, so emphasis should be placed on not letting your dog get FAT in the first place!

158

Chapter 11
Showing Your Pug

Let us assume that after a few months of tender loving care, you realize your dog is developing beyond your wildest expectations and that the dog you selected is very definitely a show dog! Of course every owner is prejudiced. But if you are sincerely interested in going to dog shows and making a champion of him, now is the time to start casting a critical eye on him from a judge's point of view.

There is no such thing as a perfect dog. Every dog has some faults, perhaps even a few serious ones. The best way to appraise your dog's degree of perfection is to compare him with the Standard for the breed, or before a judge in a show ring.

MATCH SHOWS

For the beginner there are "mock" dog shows, called Match Shows, where you and your dog go through many of the procedures of a regular dog show, but do not gain points toward championship. These shows are usually held by kennel clubs, annually or semi-annually, and much ring poise and experience can be gained there. The age limit is reduced to two or three months at match shows to give puppies three or four months of training before they compete at the regular shows when they reach six months. Many breeders evaluate their litters in this manner, choosing which is the most outgoing, which is the most poised, the best showman, etc.

For those seriously interested in showing their dogs to full championship, these match shows provide important experience for both the dog and the owner. Class categories may vary slightly,

Overleaf: Artist Francisco Ubeda Marin painted this impressive portrait of Am. Ch. Shirrayne's Golddigger for owner Tracy Williams of Sao Paolo, Brazil. Digger is handled in South America by the top handler there, Jayme B. Martinelli, and has won three Bests in Show and five Group Firsts in that country. Bred by the Shirrayne Kennels.

Above: Jap. Ch. Pugtowne's Hob-Gobblen winning at a 1969 match Show before exportation to Japan by breeder John J. Marsh. Filomena Doherty, famous breeder, and owner of Pugville Kennels, judged. **Below:** Ch. Harper's Fawn C Pants winning at the 1974 Augusta Kennel Club show under judge Michele Billings. The 15-month old bitch was handled by 14-year-old Alan L. Harper. Owned by Harper's Pugs, Jacksonville, Florida.

Left: Ch. Dougan's Silver Jo Jo, C.D.X., winning High Score in Trial at the 1st obedience trial held by the P.D.C.A. Owned and handled by Mrs. Glen Wells of Little Rock, Arkansas. **Below:** At the 1974 Mad River Valley K.C. show, judge Dr. T. Allen Kirk Jr. awarded Best of Breed to Ch. August-Goblin of Gore, and Winners Bitch and Best of Opposite Sex to Augustina-Goblin. The dogs are shown by their owners, Armin and Jane Koring.

Right; Famous Pug person Esther Wolf pictured with Ch. Wolf's Li'l Short Snort, C.D.X. Snort was grandfather of the world-famous record-breaking sire, Ch. Wolf's Li'l Joe. **Below:** Best Puppy in Show at the 1976 Manitoba, Canada show was Maranda's Karmyl of Rowann, owned and shown by Dr. and Mrs. Robert White of Lincoln, Nebraska.

according to number of entries, but basically include all the classes that are included in a regular point show. There is a nominal entry fee and, of course, ribbons and usually trophies are given as well. Unlike the point shows, entries can be made on the day of the show on the show grounds. Match shows are unbenched and provide an informal, usually congenial atmosphere for the amateur, which helps to make the ordeal of one's first adventures in the show ring a little less nerve-wracking.

THE POINT SHOWS

It is not possible to show a puppy at an American Kennel Club sanctioned point show before the age of six months. When your dog reaches this eligible age, your local kennel club can provide you with the names and addresses of the show-giving superintendents in your area who will be staging the club's dog show for them, and where you must write for an entry form.

The forms are mailed in a pamphlet called a premium list. This also includes the names of the judges for each breed, a list of the prizes and trophies, the name and address of the show-giving club and where the show will be held, as well as rules and regulations set up by the American Kennel Club which must be abided by if you are to enter.

Ch. Muse's Storm Cloud winning a Toy Group with handler Jack Funk at a Meridian, Miss. show. Owners, Dr. and Mrs. Arthur Rienetz of Chicago.

Am., Can. Ch. Ritter's Super Star finishing his Canadian title undefeated in the breed. Judge was Iris de la Torre Bueno. Bred, owned and handled by Mrs. Ferman Ritter of Sewickley, Penn.

Ch. Candy's Almond Joy pictured winning the Best of Winners and Best of Opposite Sex under veteran dog man Frank Landgraff on the way to her championship. In 1975 Joy was not only the top-rated Pug for the year, but was the # 1 Dam of all the Toy breeds according to *Kennel Review* Magazine's system.

Opp., top: Am., Can. Ch. Pugtowne's Topsy Turvey winning the 1976 P.D.C. of Greater N.Y. Specialty under Emma Stephens. Club President Al Meshirer presents the trophy. Topsy owner-handled by Gloria Camileri, Oceanside, N.Y. **Opp., bottom:** Pugtowne's Barbarella of Gore, owned by Shirley Thomas. **Above:** Ch. Pugtowne's John Bull, John J. Marsh, owner.

Ch. Bleuridges Tuffy's Button, owned by Bunny Osborn, Vero Beach, Fl. Sire was Ch. Prelly's Rolly Roister, Top Producing Pug Sire for 1969; dam was Gore's Tammy, Top Producing Pug dam for that year.

English Ch. Storm-ie of Martlesham, owned by Nancy Gifford, owner of the Martlesham Pug Kennels and president of the Pug Dog Club of England.

Ch. Peers Audie winning under Joseph Faigel. Audie was Number Two Pug in the nation in 1974, handled by Jack Potts for owners Jack and Mary Peer of Dallas. Audie was shown 61 times, and has 50 Bests of Breed and 40 Group Placements.

A booklet containing the complete set of show rules and regulations may be obtained by writing to the American Kennel Club, Inc., 51 Madison Avenue, New York, N.Y., 10010.

When you write to the Dog Show Superintendent, request not only your premium list for this particular show, but ask that your name be added to their mailing list so that you will automatically receive all premium lists in the future. List your breed or breeds and they will see to it that you receive premium lists for Specialty shows as well.

Unlike the match shows where your dog will be judged on ring behavior, at the point shows he will be judged on conformation to the breed Standard. In addition to being at least six months of age

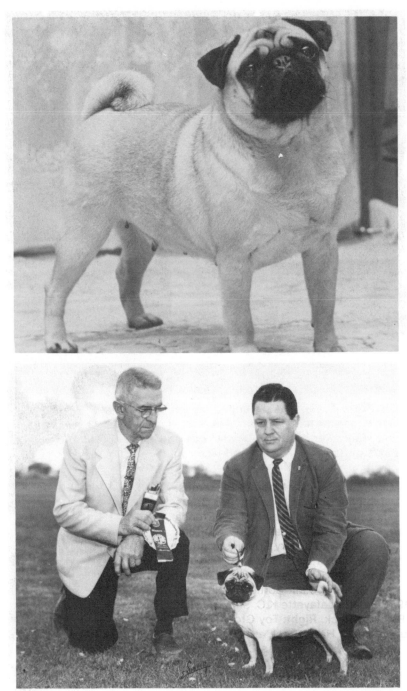

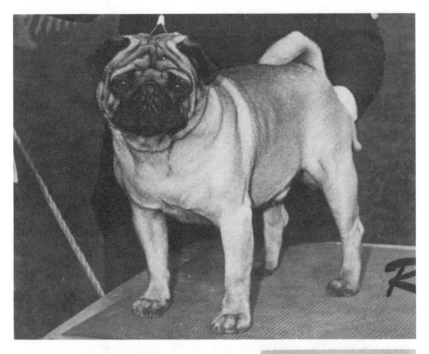

Opp., top: Dawnay Moon of Flocktons, winner of First Prize at 1976 Crufts show, bred and owned by Mrs. Brenda Banbury, Surrey England. Opp., bottom: Ch. Pugtowne's Mary Poppins winning under Luther Heisler at this 1966 dog show. John J. Marsh handling. Above: Ch. Blaylock's Mr. Softie winning at a 1966 Greater Lafayette K.C. show. Owner Rolla Blaylock. Right: Toy Group Winner under Frank Haze Burch at this 1972 Del Sur K.C. show was Ch. Blaylock's Rollicking Rolla. Mike Nemeth handled for owner Hazel Martens.

Left: Ch. Alken's John Henry of Anidee, bred and handled by Mary J. Phillips and co-owned with Gordon M. Phillips, Anidee Pugs, Shadow Hills, California. **Below:** Engl., Am., Ch. Phidigity Phircone, imported and owned by the late judge and breeder, Richard Paisley.

Above: Ch. Bleuridges Bit of Tuffy, owned by Bunny Osborn, Bleuridge Pugs, Vero Beach, Fla. **Right:** Ch. Alexander's Sump' tin F'r Nuttin, bred, owned and shown by Joan Alexander of New Orleans.

(on the day of the show) he must be a thoroughbred for a point show. This means both of his parents and he are registered with the American Kennel Club. There must be no alterations or falsifications regarding his appearance. Females cannot have been spayed and males must have both testicles in evidence. No dyes or powders may be used to enhance the appearance, and any lameness or deformity or major deviation from the Standard for the breed constitutes a disqualification.

With all these things in mind, groom your dog to the best of your ability in the area specified for this purpose in the show hall and walk into the show ring with great pride of ownership and ready for an appraisal of your dog by the judge.

The presiding judge on that day will allow each and every dog a certain amount of time and consideration before making his decisions. It is never permissible to consult the judge regarding either your dog or his decision while you are in the ring. An exhibitor never speaks unless spoken to, and then only to answer such questions as the judge may ask—the age of the dog, the dog's bite, or to ask you to move your dog around the ring once again.

However, before you reach the point where you are actually in the ring awaiting the final decisions of the judge, you will have had to decide in which of the five classes in each sex your dog should compete.

POINT SHOW CLASSES

The regular classes of the AKC are: Puppy, Novice, Bred-by-Exhibitor, American-Bred, Open; if your dog is undefeated in any of the regular classes (divided by sex) in which it is entered, he or she is **required** to enter the Winners Class. If your dog is placed second in the class to the dog which won Winners Dog or Winners Bitch, hold the dog or bitch in readiness as the judge must consider it for Reserve Winners.

Puppy Classes shall be for dogs which are six months of age and over but under twelve months, which were whelped in the U.S.A. or Canada, and which are not champions. Classes are often divided 6 and (under) 9, and 9 and (under) 12 months. The age of a dog shall be calculated up to and inclusive of the first day of a show. For example, a dog whelped on Jan. 1st is eligible to compete in a puppy class on July 1st, and may continue to compete up

174

Ch. Kropp's Stande Burt, bred by Loretta Kropp and owned by Mrs. Rolla Blaylock, and handled to this win under the late judge Haskell Schuffman by Mr. Rolla Blaylock.

175

Ch. Pugville's Mighty Wrinkles, winner of many groups and a wonderful Pug. "Pinky" was sired by Am., Can., Cuban and Bermudian Ch. Pugville's Mighty Jim ex Ch. Tarralong Sweet Amber.

Left: Ch. Bonjor's Tim Geraghty O'Weston, owned by Dr. and Mrs. Marcus M. Lowthorp of Kirkland, Wash. **Below:** Best Pug Puppy at England's Colchester Show was Lady Gemima of Ling and Flocktons. Owned by Mrs. Brenda Banbury, Flocktons Kennels, Surrey, England.

Right; Ch. Bonjor's Clara Barton, breeder-owned by Dr. Norval and Bonna Webb, Middletown, Ohio. **Below:** First Prize at 1976 Crufts Show in the Puppy Class was Dawnay Moon of Flocktons, bred and owned by Mrs. Brenda Banbury, Surrey, England.

Mai Lang XX-II with some trophies won during training with the Obedience Club of Chattanooga in 1976. Owners Dr. and Mrs. James Burchin of Nashville, Tennessee.

Ch. Nunnally's Witch Hazel finishing her title under Dr. Harry Smith. Handled by owner Louise V. Gore, Louisville, Kentucky.

Ch. Bonjor's Jim Geraghty taking a five-point major and Best of Breed at the 1st regional PDCA Specialty. Breeder Bonna Webb, owner Dr. Marcus Lowethrop.

THE PUG DOG CLUB OF AMERICA
MAY 26 1975
BEST OF WINNERS
JUDGE
MR JAMES MORAN
PHOTO BY THACKER

to and including Dec. 31st of the same year, but is not eligible to compete Jan. 1st of the following year.

The Novice Class shall be for dogs six months of age or over, whelped in the U.S.A. or Canada which have not, prior to the closing of entries, won three first prizes in the Novice Class, a first prize in Bred-by-Exhibitor, American-Bred or Open Class, nor one or more points toward a championship title.

The Bred-by-Exhibitor Class shall be for dogs whelped in the U.S.A. which are six months of age and over, which are not champions, and which are owned wholly or in part by the person or by the spouse of the person who was the breeder or one of the breeders of record. Dogs entered in the BBE Class must be handled by an owner or by a member of the immediate family of an owner, i.e., the husband, wife, father, mother, son, daughter, brother or sister.

The American-Bred Class shall be for all dogs (except champions) six months or over, whelped in the U.S.A. by reasons of a mating that took place in the U.S.A.

The Open Class is for any dog six months of age or over, except in a member specialty club show held for only American-Bred dogs, in which case the class is for American-Bred dogs only.

Winners Dog and **Winners Bitch:** After the above male classes have been judged, the first-place winners are then **required** to compete in the ring. The dog judged "Winners Dog" is awarded the points toward his championship title.

Reserve Winners are selected immediately after the Winners Dog. In case of a disqualification of a win by the AKC, the Reserve Dog moves up to "Winners" and receives the points. After all male classes are judged, the bitch classes are called.

Best of Breed or Best of Variety Competition is limited to Champions of Record or dogs (with newly acquired points, for a 90-day period prior to AKC confirmation) which have completed championship requirements, and Winners Dog and Winners Bitch (or the dog awarded Winners if only one Winners prize has been awarded), together with any undefeated dogs which have been shown only in non-regular classes; all compete for Best of Breed or Best of Variety (if the breed is divided by size, color, texture or length of coat hair, etc.).

Best of Winners: If the WD or WB earns BOB or BOV, it

181

Above: Ch. Pugtowne's Dixie Bell pictured winning the 1963 Maryland Pug Dog Club Specialty show, with her owner-handler, John J. Marsh of Oceanside, New York. Dixie is one of very few bitches to win a Pug Specialty! **Opp., top:** Ch. Sheffield's Sure-Fire shown winning Best of Opposite Sex at the 1973 Pug Dog Club of America Specialty show under judge Gordon Winders. Owned and handled by Margery Shriver of Baltimore, she is the dam of Best in Show winner, Ch. Sheffield's Dancing Tiger. Her sire was Ch. Sheffield's Sunday Punch ex Ch. Sheffield's Lucy Locket Shogo. **Opp., bottom:** Shirrayne's Okay Ozzie pictured winning the 1976 Grand Prize Sweepstakes held in conjunction with the Westchester Kennel Club show. On the left is Mrs. Elsie Sivori, judge, Mrs. Rona Rosen handler and co-owner with Mark Rosen and Mrs. Tracy Williams of Brazil, owner of the Ozzie's sire, Ch. Shirrayne's Golddigger.

BEST OF
OPPOSITE

GILBERT PHOTO

FIRST

ASHBEY PHOTO

Above: Ch. Sabbaday Kidd's Capricorn, owned by Sylvia Sidney and handled for her by Jane R. Lamarine. Breeder was Polly Lamarine. "Cappy Too" is going Best in Show at P.D.C.A. Specialty under Joan Alexander. **Opposite:** Ch. Scottie's Boy of Revonah, owned by Helen O. Bearce, Revonah Pugs, Hanson, Massachusetts. Handled by Wendell J. Sammett for this win.

automatically becomes BOW; otherwise they will be judged together for BOW (following BOB or BOV judging).

Best of Opposite Sex is selected from the remaining dogs of the opposite sex to Best of Breed or Best of Variety.

Other Classes may be approved by the AKC: **Stud Dogs, Brood Bitches, Brace Class, Team Class;** classes consisting of local dogs and bitches may also be included in a show if approved by the AKC (special rules are included in the AKC Rule Book).

The **Miscellaneous Class** shall be for purebred dogs of such breeds as may be designated by the AKC. No dog shall be eligible for entry in this class unless the owner has been granted an Indefinite Listing Privilege (ILP) and unless the ILP number is given on the entry form. Application for an ILP shall be made on a form provided by the AKC and when submitted must be accompanied by a fee set by the Board of Directors.

All Miscellaneous Breeds shall be shown together in a single class except that the class may be divided by sex if so specified in the premium list. There shall be **no** further competition for dogs entered in this class. Ribbons for 1st, 2nd, 3rd and fourth shall be Rose, Brown, Light Green and Gray, respectively. This class is open to the following Miscellaneous Breeds: Australian Cattle Dogs, Australian Kelpies, Border Collies, Cavalier King Charles Spaniels, Miniature Bull Terriers, and Spinoni Italiani.

If Your Dog Wins a Class. . .

Study the classes to make certain your dog is entered in a proper class for his or her qualifications. If your dog wins his class, the rule states: *You are required* to enter classes for Winners, Best of Breed and Best of Winners (no additional entry fees). The rule states, "No eligible dog may be withheld from competition." It is not mandatory that you stay for group judging. If *your dog wins a group,* however, *you must stay for Best-in-Show competition.*

THE PRIZE RIBBONS AND WHAT THEY STAND FOR

No matter how many entries there are in each class at a dog show, if you place first through fourth position you will receive a ribbon. These ribbons commemorate your win and can be impressive when collected and displayed to prospective buyers when

Above: Ch. Bartel's Diana winning Toy Group at the 1960 Mid-Hudson. K.C. show, 1st black Pug to take Toy Group at the time. Handler John J. Marsh, owner Florence Bartels. **Right:** Silvertown Surprise Package winning under the late Mary Pickhardt. Owned, bred, handled by Polly Lamarine.

187

Above: Shown is a faulty Pug specimen, which would be a pet-quality dog, not suited to show competition. It is shelly throughout, with incorrect muzzle, poor facial mask, lack of prominent wrinkle, an ear set too high on the skull, too long in back, has a roach back, it is too long in loin, and has poor tail carriage. Other faults: lack of substance, little forechest, over-angulated behind, sickle hocks, too straight in pastern, leggy and lacking in bone. **Below:** Another poor specimen: too heavy, too-large ears, swayback, overbuilt behind, poor tail carriage, lack of rear angulation, poor feet, down in pastern, short on leg, coarse bone.

E·H·HART

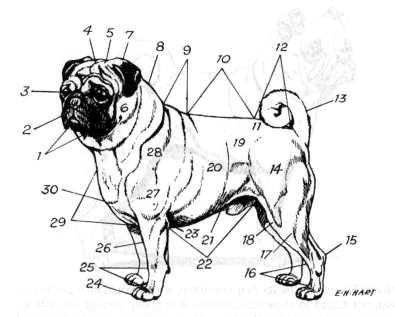

E·H·HART

Parts of the Pug

1. Underjaw	16. Metatarsus
2. Muzzle	17. Lower Thigh
3. Stop	18. Point of Stifle (Knee)
4. Skull	19. Loin
5. Occiput	20. Ribs
6. Cheek	21. Abdomen
7. Ear	22. Bottom Line
8. Neck	23. Elbow
9. Withers	24. Feet (Paws)
10. Back	25. Pastern
11. Hip	26. Forearm
12. Croup	27. Upper Arm
13. Tail (Stern)	28. Shoulder
14. Thigh	29. Forechest
15. Point of Hock	30. Prosternum

Opposite: Ch. Bonjor's Reluctant Tiger gets his just reward for winning the Toy Group at the Trenton Kennel Club show, where over 4,000 dogs were entered. Tiger was # 1 Pug Dog in America in 1974, all ratings, and was owned by June and John Benson of Florida and bred by Bonna Webb. Handled by John J. Marsh. **Above:** Ch. Ken M's Chy O'Shay pictured at a recent Kennel Club of Pasadena show with handler Ken Mulhern, who is also co-breeder and owner with Diana Mulhern of Santa Ana, Cal.

Ch. Nin Bar Hen Annabelle, English Import winning the Breed over Specials from the classes at the 1971 Staten Island Kennel Club show with owner-handler John J. Marsh.

and if you have puppies for sale, or if you intend to use your dogs at public stud.

All ribbons from the American Kennel Club licensed dog shows will bear the American Kennel Club seal, the name of the show, the date and the placement. In the classes the colors are blue for first, red for second, yellow for third, and white for fourth. Winners Dog or Winners Bitch ribbons are purple, while Reserve Dog and Reserve Bitch ribbons are purple and white. Best of Winners ribbons are blue and white; Best of Breed, purple and gold; and Best of Opposite Sex ribbons are red and white.

In the six groups, first prize is a blue rosette or ribbon, second placement is red, third yellow, and fourth white. The Best In Show rosette is either red, white and blue, or incorporates the colors used in the show-giving club's emblem.

QUALIFYING FOR CHAMPIONSHIP

Championship points are given for Winners Dog and Winners Bitch in accordance with a scale of points established by the American Kennel Club based on the popularity of the breed in entries, and the number of dogs competing in the classes. This scale of points varies in different sections of the country, but the scale is published in the front of each dog show catalog. These points may differ between the dogs and the bitches at the same show. You may, however, win additional points by winning Best of Winners, if there are fewer dogs than bitches entered, or vice versa. Points never exceed five at any one show, and a total of fifteen points must be won to constitute a championship. These fifteen points must be won under at least three different judges, and you must acquire at least two major wins. Anything from a three to five point win is a major, while one and two point wins are minor wins. Two major wins must be won under two different judges to meet championship requirements.

OBEDIENCE TRIALS

Some shows also offer Obedience Trials which are considered as separate events. They give the dogs a chance to compete and score on performing a prescribed set of exercises intended to display their training in doing useful work.

There are three obedience titles for which they may compete. First, the Companion Dog or CD title; second, the Companion Dog Excellent or CDX; and third, the Utility Dog or UD. Detailed information on these degrees is contained in a booklet entitled Official Obedience Regulations and may be obtained by writing to the American Kennel Club.

JUNIOR SHOWMANSHIP COMPETITION

Junior Showmanship Competition is for boys and girls in different age groups handling their own dogs or one owned by a member of their immediate family. There are four divisions: *Novice Junior,* for the boys and girls at least ten years of age and less than 13; *Novice Senior,* for boys and girls at least 13 and under 17. The Novice divisions are for those who have not won three first place awards in a Novice class at a licensed or member show. The *Open Junior* is for boys and girls at least ten and under 13; the

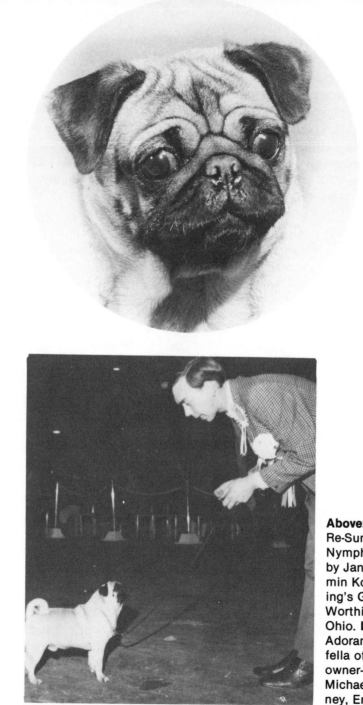

Above: Cathay-Re-Summer Nymph, owned by Jane and Armin Koring, Koring's Goblins, Worthington, Ohio. **Left:** Ch. Adoram Cinderfella of Pallas, owner-handler Michael Quinney, England.

Ch. Jolley Li'l Peter Punkinhead pictured winning a four-point major on the way to his championship at the 1976 Vancouver Kennel Club show under judge Mrs. Victor Olmos-Ollivier. Peter is owned and handled by Paul R. Jolley, of Seattle, Washington.

Left; Ch. Blaylock's Gingersnap, owner-handled by Hazel Martens. **Below:** Ch. Hazelbridge Frog, owned by Creighton Jackson, Jackpot Pugs, Spring, Texas.

Above: Int. Ch. Flocktons Gay Caballero, owned by Madam Mortal, Montrono, France. **Right:** Ch. Gore's Sir Flip, owned by Louise V. Gore.

Left: Ch. Candy's Mr. Teddy Bear winning Group Fourth at a 1969 dog show. Mrs. Muriel Dusek, owner; handler, John J. Marsh. **Below:** Goodwin's John-Boy winning on the way to championship at the 1976 P.D.C. of Greater N.Y. Bred, owned and handled by Shirley J. Goodwin.

Right: Paragon's Page of Wisselwood is going Best of Breed from the classes under Frank Oberstar at a 1976 show. Owned and handled by Linda Ermlich Hart, Versailles, Ohio. **Below:** Ch. Sheffield's Sally Sunshine winning the Breed under judge A. Peter Knoop at a 1972 show. Owned by Linda Ermlich Hart.

PUG DOG CLUB
GREATER NEW YORK
FEBRUARY 9, 1975
BEST
JUNIOR
HANDLER
A BUSHMAN PHOTO

Opp., top: Best Junior Handler at the 1975 Pug Dog Club of America show in New York was Robert Aldrich of Pelham, Mass. Judge Ruth Turner made the award to Robert and his dog, Am., Can. Ch. Ted's Kauffee Royal Rupert. **Opp., bottom:** Ch. Dandy's Toastmaster finishing for championship at the 1972 Spartenburg K.C. show. Handler E. Mangles for owner Shirley Tackett of Lutz, Florida. **Above:** Ch. Blaylock's Little Twiggie, Best of Opposite Sex winner at the 1969 City of Angels Pug Specialty from the classes over Specials. Owned by Hazel Martens, Larimar Ranch Kennels, San Diego, California.

J. Stan Johnson, age five years, with Mi Billy Boy of MSJ, waiting their turn in the show ring. Actually, Stan will have to wait a few years yet before he can actually compete as a junior exhibitor.

Open Senior is for those at least 13 and under 17. The Open divisions are for those who have won three first place awards in a Novice Junior Showmanship Class at a licensed or member show.

As Junior Showmanship Competition at the dog shows increased in popularity, certain changes and improvements had to be made. As of July 1, 1978, the American Kennel Club issued a new booklet containing the regulations for Junior Showmanship which may be obtained by writing to the AKC at 51 Madison Avenue, New York, 10010. It was amended in June, 1979.

DOG SHOW PHOTOGRAPHERS

Every show has at least one official photographer who will be more than happy to take a photograph of your dog with the judge, ribbons and trophies, along with you or your handler. These make marvelous remembrances of your top show wins and are frequently framed along with the ribbons for display purposes. Photographers can be paged at the show over the public address system, if you wish to obtain this service. Prices vary, but you will probably find it costs little to capture these happy moments, and the photos can always be used in the various dog magazines to advertise your dog's wins.

TWO TYPES OF DOG SHOWS

There are two types of dog shows licensed by the American Kennel Club. One is the all-breed show which includes classes for all the recognized breeds, and groups of breeds; i.e., all terriers, all toys, etc. Then there are the specialty shows for one particular breed which also offer championship points.

BENCHED OR UNBENCHED DOG SHOWS

The show-giving clubs determine, usually on the basis of what facilities are offered by their chosen show site, whether their show will be benched or unbenched. A benched show is one where the dog show superintendent supplies benches (cages for toy dogs). Each bench is numbered and its corresponding number appears on your entry identification slip which is sent to you prior to the show date. The number also appears in the show catalog. Upon entering the show you should take your dog to the bench where he should remain until it is time to groom him before entering the

Ch. Mar-Los Knick-Knack going Winners Bitch and Best of Opposite Sex under judge James Trullinger at a 1976 show. Thomas Okun handled for owner Charles J. Brown of the Bronx, New York. Knick-Knack finished her championship at this show.

BEST OF OPPOSITE

GILBERT PHOTO

Opposite: Ch. Pug Haven's Man About South pictured winning Best of Breed at the 1962 Saw Mill River Kennel Club show, handled by John J. Marsh for the famous Pug Haven Kennels in Florida. **Above:** Ch. Fahey's Friendly wins the Toy Group at the 1976 Ozarks Kennel Club show under judge Mrs. James Carter. The sire was Alava Wee Willie ex Ch. Fahey's Allafire. Owned, bred and shown by Mrs. Lee Fahey of Kansas City, Missouri.

ring to be judged. After judging, he must be returned to the bench until the official time of dismissal from the show. At an unbenched show the club makes no provision whatsoever for your dog other than an enormous tent (if an outdoor show) or an area in a show hall where all crates and grooming equipment must be kept.

Benched or unbenched, the moment you enter the show grounds you are expected to look after your dog and have it under complete control at all times. This means short leads in crowded aisles or getting out of cars. In the case of a benched show, a "bench chain" is needed. It should allow the dog to move around, but not get down off the bench. It is also not considered cute to have small tots leading enormous dogs around a dog show where the child might be dragged into the middle of a dog fight.

PROFESSIONAL HANDLERS

If you are new in the fancy and do not know how to handle your dog to his best advantage, or if you are too nervous or physically unable to show your dog, you can hire a professional handler who will do it for a specified fee. The more successful or well-known handlers charge higher rates, but generally speaking there is a pretty uniform charge for this service. As the dog progresses with his wins in the ring, the fee increases proportionately. Included in this service is professional advice on when and where to show the dog, grooming, a statement of your wins at each show, and all trophies and ribbons that the dog accumulates. Any cash award is kept by the handler as a sort of bonus.

When engaging a handler, it is advisable to select one that does not take more dogs to a show that he can properly and comfortably handle. You want your dog to receive his individual attention and not be rushed into the ring at the last moment, because the handler has been busy with too many other dogs in other rings. Some handlers require that you deliver the dog to their establishment a few days ahead of the show so they have ample time to groom and train him. Others will accept well-behaved and previously trained and groomed dogs at ringside, if they are familiar with the dog and the owner. This should be determined well in advance of the show date. NEVER expect a handler to accept a dog at ringside that is not groomed to perfection!

There are several sources for locating a professional handler.

Dog magazines carry their classified advertising; a note or telephone call to the American Kennel Club will put you in touch with several in your area. Usually, you will be billed after the day of the show.

DO YOU REALLY NEED A HANDLER?

The answer to the above question is sometimes yes! However, the answer most exhibitors give is, "But I can't *afford* a professional handler!" or, "I want to show my dog myself. Does that mean my dog will never do any big winning?"

Do you *really* need a handler to win? If you are mishandling a good dog that should be winning and isn't, because it is made to

Ch. Bonjor's Different Drummer winning the Breed at the Pug Specialty of Greater New York show held in conjunction with the Westchester event in September 1976. This prestigious win was made under judge Joseph Rowe. John Marsh handled for owners Mr. and Mrs. H.L. Benninger of Parkersburg, West Va. Club President Al Meshirer presents the trophy.

Opposite: Am., Can. Ch. Sabbaday Favor winning Best of Opposite Sex at the 1972 Progressive Dog Club show. Owner-handled by Polly J. Lamarine. **Above:** Am., Can. Ch. Pug Pen's Captain Midnight, owned by Sylvia Sidney and handled by Jane R. Lamarine. Cappy is pictured winning the Breed under the late Mary Shipman Pickhardt at a 1967 show.

Left: Canadian Ch. Kendoric's Li'l China Star, C.D. winning Best of Opposite Sex at the 1975 Woodstock K.C. show under Wilma Hunter. Owner Doris Aldrich of Pelham, Mass. **Below:** Ch. Plevalis Primo of Gore winning the Breed with handler Donald Foral, who co-owns with Roger Perry.

Right: Sin Chen's Trace of Tarr winning in 1976. Owned by Susan and Gary Karp of Washington, D.C. Susan is handling here. **Below:** Ch. Broughcastl Balladeer winning Best of Breed from the classes over 26 Specials at the 1975 Westminster show under Anne Rogers Clark. Handled by Douglas Huffman; co-breeder Dr. Norval Webb completes the picture.

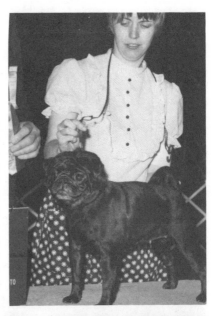

Ch. Anidee's Re-Pete won at the 1975 Santa Barbara K.C. show under James P. Cavallaro. This was the third year in a row Re-Pete had a Best of Breed win at this show! Owner-handled and bred by Mary J. Phillips, Anidee Pugs, Shadow Hills, California.

The Duchess of Windsor and Filomena Doherty with the Duchess's
new Pug, Ch. Pugvilles Imperial Imp II, sired by Mrs. Doherty's Am.,
Can., Cuban and Bermudian Champion Pugville's Mighty Jim.

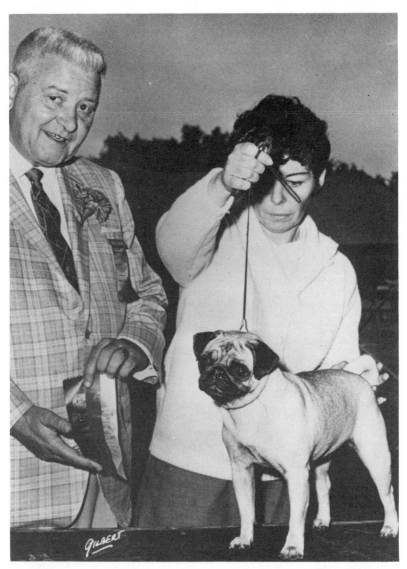

Ch. Candy's Vanilla Fudge, owner-handled to her championship by Muriel Dusek of Norfolk, Connecticut. "Fugie" was Best of Winners for a five-point major at a Pug Dog Club of Maryland Specialty show.

look simply terrible in the ring by its owner, the answer is yes. If you don't know how to handle a dog properly, why make your dog look bad when a handler could show it to its best advantage? Some owners simply cannot handle a dog well and still wonder why their dogs aren't winning in the ring, no matter how hard they try. Others are nervous and this nervousness travels down the leash to the dog and the dog behaves accordingly. Some people are extroverts by nature, and these are the people who usually make excellent handlers. Of course, the biggest winning dogs at the shows usually have a lot of "show off" in their nature, too, and this helps a great deal.

THE COST OF CAMPAIGNING
A DOG WITH A HANDLER

Many champions are shown an average of 25 times before completing a championship. In entry fees at today's prices, that adds up to at least $200. This does not include motel bills, traveling expenses, or food. There have been dog champions finished in fewer shows, say five to ten shows, but this is the exception rather than the rule. When and where to show should be thought out carefully so that you can perhaps save money on entries. Here is one of the services a professional handler provides that can mean a considerable saving. Hiring a handler can save money in the long run if you just wish to make a champion. If your dog has been winning reserves and not taking the points and a handler can finish him in five to ten shows, you would be ahead financially. If your dog is not really top quality, the length of time it takes even a handler to finish it (depending upon competition in the area) could add up to a large amount of money.

Campaigning a show specimen that not only captures the wins in his breed but wins group and Best in Show awards gets up into the big money. To cover the nation's major shows and rack up a record as one of the top dogs in the nation usually costs an owner between ten and fifteen thousand dollars a year. This includes not only the professional handler's fees for taking the dog into the ring, but the cost of conditioning and grooming, board, advertising in the dog magazines, photographs, etc.

There is great satisfaction in winning with your own dog, especially if you have trained and cared for it yourself. With

218

Opposite: Ch. Sabbaday's Cinnamin Candy winning with John Marsh. Owner, Mrs. Muriel Dusek, Norfolk, Conn. **Right:** Ch. Pugholm's Little Betty Blue, top bitch on the Pacific Coast for 1957, 1958 and 1959. She is pictured finishing her championship under the late, highly-respected breeder - judge, E.E. Ferguson. Owner-handler Hazel Martens. **Below:** Ch. SBK's Jackpots Bingo, bred and owned by Creighton Jackson and Myrtle Landry, Spring, Texas.

Ch. Sabbaday Full of It, owned, bred and shown by Polly J. Lamarine, Silvertown Pugs. Junior is a son of Am. and Can. Ch. Sabbaday Captain's Kidd and Am. and Can. Ch. Sabbaday Favor. Photo by D. Perzan.

Opposite: Ch. Stonecrusher of Wisselwood pictured winning Best of Breed at the 1973 Sundusky Kennel Club show. Stonecrusher is bred, owned and handled by Lorene Vickers, of Beach City, Ohio.

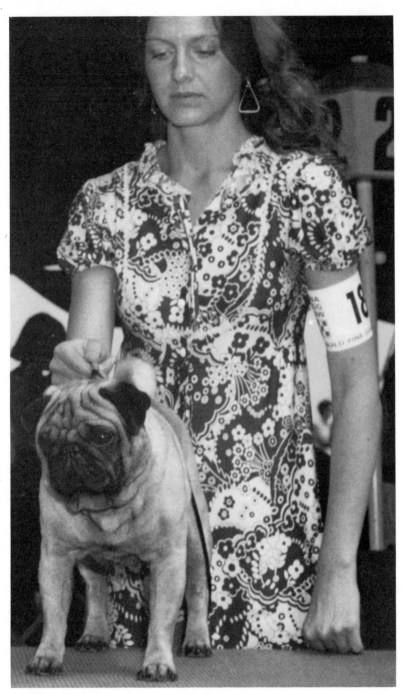

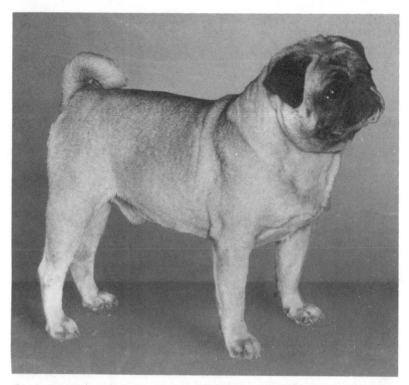

Ch. Laja's Blastoff Duke, champion in America, Canada, and Mexico. He is owned by Mimi Keller, editor and publisher of *Pug Talk* Magazine of Dallas, Texas.

today's enormous entries at the dog shows and so many worthy dogs competing for top wins, many owners who said "I'd rather do it myself!" and meant it became discouraged and eventually hired a handler anyway.

However, if you really are in it just for the sport, you can and should handle your own dog if you want to. You can learn the tricks by attending training classes, and you can learn a lot by carefully observing the more successful professional handlers as they perform in the ring. Model yourself after the ones that command respect as being the leaders in their profession. But, if you find you'd really rather be at ringside looking on, then do get a handler so that your worthy dog gets his deserved recognition in the ring. To own a good dog and win with it is a thrill, so good luck, no matter how you do it.

Chapter 12
The Pug in Obedience

St. Mathilde's Prayer

O God,
Give unto me by grace
that obedience which thou hast
given to my little dog
by nature.

TRAINING YOUR PUG

There are few things in the world a dog would rather do than please his master. Therefore, obedience training, even the very basic training, will be a pleasure for your Pug, if taught correctly, and will make him a much nicer animal to live with the rest of his life.

EARLY TRAINING AT HOME

Some breeders start training their puppies as early as two weeks of age. At this time, or shortly thereafter, they place a ¼-inch ribbon around the puppy's neck, so loose that you can get two fingers in it, and leave it on for various periods of the day. Also leave about one inch of ribbon on the end so the puppy can pull on it and feel the pressure of the pull on its neck and become accustomed to it. This very early exposure will help the puppy adjust to a collar and lead when the time comes for the official leash training and obedience work.

If you intend to show your puppy there are other formalities you can observe as early as four weeks of age that will also accustom the puppy to future show training. One of the most important points is setting him up on a table in show stance. Make it short

Ch. Pugville's Dream Girl, sired by Am., Can., Cuban and Bda. Ch. Pugville's Mighty Jim ex Ch. Oya's Toffee. Photographed by Tauskey.

Right: Tex McCreary was trophy presenter at the 1959 P.D.C.A. Specialty. Accepting for owner Otto Rosenberg is handler John Marsh. Judge was Pug breeder-owner James W. Trullinger. The winning dog was named Captain Chris. **Below:** Ch. Ivanwold Gayberry Carolina winning the Grand Prize Sweepstakes at the 1973 Pug Dog Club of Greater New York Specialty. The judge was Dr. Arthur H. Reinitz; presenting the trophy is Al Meshirer. She is owned by Dr. and Mrs. Edward Patterson.

Above: Ch. Higman's Little Heller pictured winning the Toy Group at the 1972 Texas Kennel Club show under judge Henry Stoecker. Owned by Ron and Shari Higman of Miami, Florida. **Opp., top:** The Duke and Duchess of Windsor present the trophies at the 1958 P.D.C.A. Specialty. The top award went to Ch. Blaylock's Mar-Ma-Duke, owned by Gordon Winders of Skokie, Ill. His handler is Jack Funk, the judge was Walter C. Foster. On the right is Winners Bitch and Best of Opposite Sex winner Minuet of Puglen, owned by Janet S. Kosvic of Elizabeth, N.J. **Opp., bottom:** Ch. Heislers Hankey Boy, taking a Best of Breed win under the late and respected judge, Richard Paisley. Hank was handled by John Marsh for owners Ruth and Clifford Meeks of Wenonah, N.J.

227

and sweet, make it a sort of game, but repeatedly place the puppy in a show stance and hold him that way while giving lavish praise. After a few weeks of doing this a few times each day, you will find the puppy takes to the idea of "stand" and "stay" very readily. It will be a big help in future show training.

WHEN TO START FORMAL TRAINING

Official training should not start until the puppy is about six months of age. However, as the puppy grows along the way, you should certainly get him used to his name, to come when he is called, the meaning of "come," and "no," and other basic commands. Repetition is the answer, with plenty of patience, since the Pug is a strong-willed dog even as a puppy and will probably prefer to

Reba Weitz' American and Canadian C.D. title holder, bred by Harriette Rappaport of Flushing, New York.

Bohemian Joey of Kae-Jac, a Companion Dog owned by Doris Aldrich of Pelham, Massachusetts.

play his way through those first carefree six months of life. If your dog is to be a show dog he must also learn to "stand" and "stay."

THE REWARD METHOD

The only acceptable kind of training is the kindness and reward method which will build a strong bond between dog and master. You want to establish respect and attention, not fear and punishment. Give each command, preceded by his name, and make it stick. Do not move on to another command or lesson until the first one is mastered. Train where there are no distractions at first, and never when the dog is tired, right after eating, or for too long a period. When his interest wanes, quit until another session later in the day. Two or three sessions a day with a bright dog, increasing the time from, say, five minutes to fifteen might do. Each dog is different and you must set your own schedule with your own dog.

Above: Eng. Ch. Hoonme
Invictus, owned by Mrs. A.
Williams, Hoonme Pugs,
Wilts, England. **Left:** Ch.
Shirrayne's Brash Buffie,
handled by breeder-
owner Shirley Thomas.

Right: Ch. Goodwin's Autumn Gold, breeder-owned by Shirley J. Goodwin of St. Petersburg, Fla. **Below:** Ch. Dhandy's Goodwin Daffodil, owned by Shirley Tackett of Lutz, Florida.

231

Above: Ch. Shirrayne's
Bashful Biff winning under
James Trullinger. Handler-
breeder-owner, Shirley
Thomas. **Left:** Ch. Lilliput's
Cracker Jack, handled by Pat
McManus for owner Louise
Anderson of Derby, Conn.

Above: Ch. Elfin of Hazelbridge, owned by Mrs. A. Ansell, Pughall Pugs, London. Mrs. Ansell prefers the blacks, and is particularly proud of Elfin's magnificent head. Photo by Diane Pearce. **Below:** Winning combination ... brother and sister win Winners Dog and Winners Bitch: The fawn dog is Ch. Anidee's Re-Pete, and the black bitch Ch. Anidee's Dark Secret. Breeder-owner Gordon M. Phillips, Shadow Hills, Calif.

The fantastic Lord Percival of Wessex, an American, Bermudian, Canadian and Mexican C.D.X. owned, trained and handled by Patricia Scully of Suffern, N.Y. Percy was the first Pug to be shown in Mexico and was the first C.D.X. Pug in Mexico.

WHAT YOU NEED TO START TRAINING

The soft nylon show leads available at all pet stores are best for early training. Later, perhaps a metal-like choke chain can be used. Let the puppy play with the lead, or even carry it around, when you first put it on. Too much pressure pulling at the end of it is liable to get him off to a bad start. You don't want the collar to seem like a harness.

FORMAL SCHOOL TRAINING

The yellow pages of your phone book can lead you to dog training schools or classes for official training along with other dogs. Usually they want the puppies to be six months of age, but you might start making inquiries at around four months. If you intend to show your dog this early training is very important. If you don't intend to show your dog it will still make him easier to live with and do credit to the breed, as well as to both of you!

OBEDIENCE DEGREES

There are several obedience titles recognized by the AKC, that

234

dogs may earn through a process of completed exercises. The Companion Dog, or C.D. degree is divided into three classes: Novice, Open and Utility, with a total score of 200. After the dog has qualified with a score of at least 170 points or better he has earned the right to include the letters C.D. after his name and is eligible to compete in Open Class competition to earn a Companion Dog Excellent Degree, or C.D.X., after his name. After qualifying in three shows for this title he may compete for the Utility Dog title, or U.D. initials after his name. Complete information on the exercises may be obtained by writing to the AKC in New York.

THE NEW OBEDIENCE TRIAL
CHAMPIONSHIP TITLES

The Board of Directors of the American Kennel Club has approved the following addition to the Obedience Regulations, effective July 1, 1977.

Chapter 2A
Obedience Trial Championship

Section 1. Dogs that May Compete.
Championship points will be recorded only for those dogs which have earned the Utility Dog Title. Any dog that has been awarded the title of Obedience Trial Champion may continue to compete, and if such a dog earns a First or Second place ribbon, that dog shall also earn the points.

Section 2. Championship Points.
Championship points will be recorded for those dogs which have earned a First or Second place ribbon competing in the Open B or Utility Class (or Utility B, if divided), according to the schedule of points established by the Board of Directors of The American Kennel Club. In counting the number of eligible dogs in competition, a dog that is disqualified, or is dismissed, excused or expelled from the ring by the judge shall not be included.

Left: J Par's Fat Albert, pictured with handler Shirley A. Daigle; the judge is Dorothy Nickles. Owner Jean Parsons, J Par's Pugs, Houston. **Below:** Am., Can. Ch. Sabbaday Captain's Kidd, owned by Sylvia Sidney and handled by co-owner Jane R. Lamarine.

Right: Ch. Gentleman's Purpose, owned by Jean L. Parsons. Judge here is Olive E. Laver. **Below:** Adorian Dacifar, home-bred by owner Michael Quinney of Cambridge, England.

Top Pug in the United States for 1967 was American and Canadian Champion Miller's Imperial Drum Major, owner-handled by Hazel Martens, and undefeated in his quest for championship.

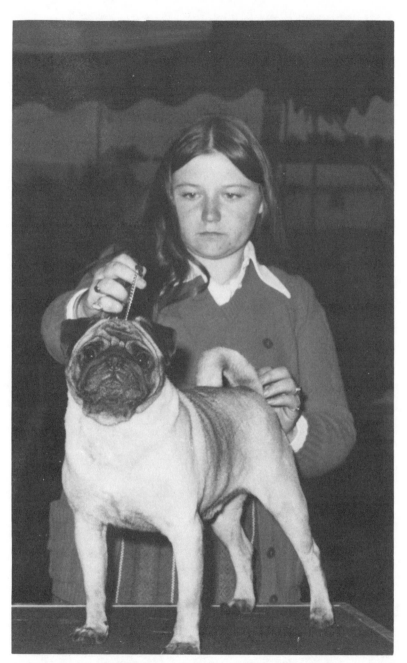

Another fine Sabbaday Pug—the one shown here at a recent event is Champion Sabbaday Pickpocket, handled by Polly Lamarine.

Requirements for the Obedience Trial Champion
are as follows:

1. Shall have won 100 points; and
2. shall have won a First place in Utility (or Utility B, if divided) provided there are at least three dogs in competition; and
3. shall have won a First place in Open B, provided there are at least six dogs in competition; and
4. shall have won a third First place under the conditions of 2 or 3 above; and
5. shall have won these three First places under three different judges.

Section 3. O.T. Ch. Title Certificate.

The American Kennel Club will issue an Obedience Trial Championship Certificate for each registered dog and will permit the use of the letters O.T. Ch. preceding the name of each dog that meets these requirements.

Julie M. Phillips with Anidee's Black Magic, C.D. and judge Milton E. Gibian on the day Magic finished for her C.D. degree at the 1973 Santa Barbara Kennel Club show.

Ch. Wolf's Hondo Sahib, C.D.X., famous show and obedience dog of the 1950's, exhibits his perfect jumping form while doing open obedience work. Owned by Esther Wolf of Omaha.

Section 4. Ineligibility and Cancellation.

If an ineligible dog has been entered in any licensed or member obedience trial or dog show, or if the name of the owner given on the entry form is not that of the person or persons who actually owned the dog at the time entries closed, or if shown in a class for which it had not been entered, or if its entry form is deemed invalid or unacceptable by the American Kennel Club, all resulting awards shall be cancelled. In computing the championship points, such ineligible dogs, whether or not they have received awards, shall be counted as having competed.

Section 5. Move Ups.

If an award in any of the regular classes is cancelled, the next highest scoring dog shall be moved up and the award to the dog moved up shall be counted the same as if it had been the original award. If there is no dog of record to move up, the award shall be void.

The English import Ch. Martlesham Galahad of Bournle, owned by the late breeder-judge Richard Paisley.

Ch. King Zarak, owned by Sue Ann Felsen of Brooklyn, New York.

Trifle of Martlesham and the black Tomerans Brenda, owned by Mrs. Phoebe Springall of Devon, England.

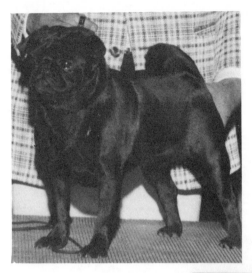

Am., Can. Ch. Rowann's Cinderella, co-owned by Dr. Robert White and his wife.

Ch. Paulaine's Dr. Peppar, owned by Paul V. Lipka, La Jolla, California.

Ch. Candy's Golden Taffy, owned by Muriel Dusek of Norfolk, Connecticut.

Left; Ch. Bill's Patchen Boy of Larimar, one of the top show winners of the Larimar Ranch Kennels of Hazel Martens. **Below:** Ch. Dandy's Doryble Kippi, C.D., winning in the conformation ring under the late judge Marjorie Seiburn. Co-owned by Mrs. Paul Kaspar, handling, and Mrs. W.J. Braley.

Right: Ch. Bonjors Sally Rand, owned by Bonna Webb. **Below:** Cricket Miss of Larimar, C.D., owned and trained by Hazel Martens.

Left: Shirrayne's Doodlebug winning at the 1973 Plainfield K.C. show under George Fowler. Owned by Dr. and Mrs. Robert L. Gossweiler. **Below:** Ch. Nazrep Chingachgook, owned and bred by Lucille Perzan, finishes championship here. Breeder-judge Joseph Rowe presents ribbon.

Right: Am., Can., Mex. Ch. Glenray's It's A Wonder, in the 1960's. Handled by owner Mary J. Phillips. **Below:** Ch. Greentubs Busy Bee finishing championship under late breeder-judge, Richard Paisley in March 1973. This lovely English import has been a major brood bitch at Shirley Thomas' Shirrayne Kennels.

Jo Jo goes over the high jump, demonstrating the correct form that was partly responsible for his attaining the C.D.X. title. owned by Glen Wells of Little Rock, Arkansas.

Section 6. Return of Awards.

If the win of a dog shall be cancelled by The American Kennel Club, the owner of the dog shall return all ribbons and prizes to the show-giving club within ten days of receipt of the notice of cancellation from The American Kennel Club.

Section 7. Point Schedule.

UTILITY CLASS

Number Competing	Points For First Place	Points For Second Place	Number Competing	Points For First Place	Points For Second Place
6-10	2	0	3-5	2	0
11-15	4	1	6-9	4	1
16-20	6	2	10-14	6	2
21-25	10	3	15-19	10	3
26-30	14	4	20-24	14	4
31-35	18	5	25-29	18	5
36-40	22	7	30-34	22	7
41-45	26	9	35-39	26	9
46-50	30	11	40-44	30	11
51-56	34	13	45-48	34	13

PUG DOG CLUB OBEDIENCE AWARD

The first year the Pug Dog Club of America received an application for their highest average obedience score award was 1962. The honor went to Button's Little Lottie, C.D. who had an average of 198⅓ for a total score of 595 out of a possible 600 points. Lottie's owner and trainer was Mrs. Bonham B. Barton, a new member to the parent club.

In 1964 Little Lottie again won the club's obedience award, this time for the highest average score of 194½ while earning her Utility Dog degree. This was also the first U.D. title won by a club member's Pug.

OTHER PUG AWARD WINNERS

The number of Pugs which have won Companion Dog titles are too numerous to list here. While it seems a shame they cannot all be included, it is encouraging to know that so many of our breed qualify in the obedience as well as the show ring. The same holds true for Pugs which have earned titles in more than one country such as Canada and Mexico and Pugs which have won their C.D.X. titles.

We are aware also that a few Pugs have earned their U.D. titles along with Little Lottie mentioned earlier, and one Pug has now captured the Tracking Dog degree.

Chapter 13
The Pug in Art And Literature

It is not difficult to understand the tremendous number of pieces in countless collections devoted to the Pug, when you realize that the breed has been popular for so many centuries. Replicas of the Pug have been produced in just about every known medium and art form known to the art world down through the years.

In the art world perhaps the first known reproductions of the Pug were old Chinese paintings found in the Imperial Dog Book by artist Tsou Yi-Kwei who lived from 1686 to 1766. Another early artifact was the Jean-Baptiste Audrey picture portraying Louis XV's favorite Pug dog in 1730. This picture hangs in the Lille Museum in France. However, a painting of George III playing cards dating back to around 1800 shows a Pug, and was rendered by Albrecht de Vriendt, a Belgian artist.

One of the first Dutch artists to gain fame who included Pugs in his master works was painter William Hogarth (1697-1764). He owned two Pugs, the first in 1730 named Pugg, believed to be the Pug that appears in his The House of Cards, and strutting in The Strode Family, a painting he did in 1738. Pugg was lost at one point in his life with the artist and Hogarth was so depressed by his disappearance that he inserted an advertisement in the Sunday, December 5, 1730 edition of *The Craftsman* newspaper which read as follows:

LOST
"From the Broad Cloth Warehouse, in the Little Piazza, Covent Garden, a light-colour'd Dutch DOG, with black Muzzle, and answers to the Name of Pugg. Whoever has found him, and will

Opposite: Said to be the most beautiful painting featuring a Pug . . . *The Marquesa de Pontejos,* by Francisco de Goya, (1746-1828) is part of the Andrew Mellon Collection at the National Gallery of Art in Washington, D.C.

Above: Pug models from around the world collected by C.A. Veldhuis of the Netherlands. All are approximately 100 years old. **Left:** Two Pug pieces from James Moran's collection. **Below:** A famous classic painting of three little girls at tea with their Pug dog, seen at the left.

252

Above: Ceramic plates created by Carol Schmidt of Bellmore, N.Y. **Right:** Carol Moorland Marshall's rendering of a typical show-quality Pug dog. **Below:** A painting entitled *Playing* by Schimler, dated 1872, courtesy of Helen Bortner of Baltimore.

bring him to Mr. Hogarth, at the said place, shall have half a Guinea reward."

Perhaps Pugg was never returned, for Mr. Hogarth's second Pug was immortalized on canvas in 1740. His name was Trump and he is the dog included in Hogarth's self-portrait entitled, The Painter and his Pug, which hangs in the Tate Gallery in London.

Ronald Paulson's book entitled *Hogarth: His Life, Art and Times,* published by the Yale University Press contains an interesting report on Hogarth's, "The Painter and His Pug". . . .

"His self-portrait is on an oval canvas resting on a pile of books, the works of Swift, Shakespeare and Milton; these are flanked by his alter ego, the bluff, honest-faced Pug, and his painter's palette. The painting is built up in Hogarth's usual way; he must have begun it as a simple self-portrait, then painted the dog as an afterthought (some red of his smock shows through). His black waistcoat (under the red smock) was originally a white ruffle, and the fur cap was at first a bonnet of some sort. The dog and the

An engraving of Dutch Pugs by G. Lance, dated 1836. The engraving was done from a painting by W.R. Lumilla. Courtesy of Helen Bortner.

Actual posed photograph of a tail-cropping in 1897, courtesy of Helen Bortner.

other symbolic objects are placed with reversal and engraving in mind; one is to read up through the Pug to Hogarth (both looking to the right) and then to the palette and the books. Even Hogarth's prominent scar is moved in the print so it will remain on the right side of his forehead. Thus Hogarth give us his own face and the no-nonsense Pug to explain it. In the art treatises, old masters were characterized by animals—Michelangelo by a dragon, Leonardo DaVinci by a lion, Titian by an ox. Hogarth draws mockingly on that tradition. The Pug, who appeared as a trademark in several of his works prior to the self-portrait, is also a satiric mask representing the artist's watchdog function and his moral toughness, reminiscent of Fielding's "Captain Hercules Vinegar."

There is also on view at The British Museum Paul Sandby's *Burlesque sur le Burlesque,* done in 1753, a satirical sketch of

Bisque candle sticks, old Wedgewood chip and dip dish and a crystal compote, all featuring Pugs and part of Helen Bortner's vast collection.

An oil painting of a Pug by Wally Denton and some ceramics made by Diana Mulhern, Santa Rosa.

One of actress Sylvia Sidney's original needlepoint designs featuring a black Pug, created in the image of one of her own dogs.

A rare piece: a wooden dog house with an emerging Pug dog on a chain. From the collection owned by the Rowann Kennels, Lincoln, Nebraska.

A photographic reproduction of an old victorian Christmas Card by
C.D. Kenny, courtesy of Helen Bortner.

Above: a close-up of the mantelpiece at the home of actress Sylvia Sidney, showing her display of treasured pieces of Pug statuary, paintings and memorabilia. **Below:** A most unusual trio of figurines from James Moran's collection. Most interesting is the statuette in the center, of a Pug wearing a top hat. The smallest figurine is of a girl with her Pug dog in her lap; the third depicts a Pug gazing skyward.

Hogarth and his pugs. Two of Hogarth's close political friends, John Wilkes and Charles Churchill, curate of St. John the Evangelist's at Millbank, were also political satirists. Churchill did a satirical piece called "Epistle to William Hogarth," and Hogarth replied with his "Pug's Reply to Parson Bruin," in which he depicted the image of Churchill as that of a bear in clerical bands, opposed by a small Hogarthian Pug. This sketch is in the British Museum's collection and also appears in Ronald Paulson's book.

In 1740, the same year the self-portrait was done, Hogarth's friend, Louis Francois Roubiliac sculpted a terra cotta bust of Hogarth along with a companion statue of Trump. A porcelain copy of Trump's statue can be seen at the Victoria and Albert Museum in London.

Mrs. Hogarth also was fond of Pugs and one of her Pugs is buried at the end of the walk in their garden at Chiswick. Hogarth himself carved the epitaph in the tombstone which read, "Life to the last enjoyed, here Pompey lies."

A very old piano baby with Pug from the collection of James Moran. This charming piece is just one of many interesting Pug figurines and statuettes in Mr. Moran's collection.

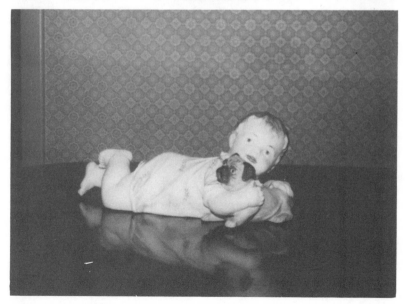

A painting by I.H. Beard, entered according to an act of Congress in the office of the Librarian of Congress, Washington, D.C. in 1880 by M. Knoedler and Company. Courtesy Helen Bortner.

This painting by Breton Riviere is entitled *Envy, Hatred, and Malice.* Note the anxious Pug mother in lower left hand corner, and the Pug puppy being safely held aloft in the girl's grasp. This interesting painting was photographed for our book by Helen Bortner.

Ch. Anidee's Curlie Cutie shown in 1952 with ribbons and trophies won during her show career. Cutie was one of the early Pugs for the Anidee Kennels of Mary J. and Gordon M. Phillips.

William H. Hopkins, famous artist who portrayed Queen Victoria and the Prince Consort in paintings dating back to 1880, produced this oil on canvas entitled *The Artist's Dog "Pug."*

Above: Pugs at play, owned by Rowann Kennels, Lincoln, Neb. **Left:** Four old ceramic Pugs: clay Pug from China on the right, and, **Below:** on the left is an Elbogan Pug; center, a Pug from Scotland; and on the right an old Bisque Pug figurine. All are from James Moran's collection.

Above: An oriental Pug dog of glazed earthenware from the Chinese Chi'en Lung period, circa 1725. Courtesy C.A. Veldhuis, the Netherlands. **Below:** A pair of Vincennes Pug dogs, circa 1753, 5½" tall. The seated figures of a male and a female Pug dog with a nursing puppy is in soft paste. Each wears a collar with bells and is seated on an oblong base with leaves and berries. The pair, on display at the New York Gallery, is valued in excess of $10,000. Photo courtesy of the Antique Porcelain Company of London, New York and Zurich.

OTHER ARTISTS OF THE PUG

A drawing of a Pug entitled "Le Dougin" by F. Chereau appeared in 1750, and the famous Goya painting "La Marquesa de Pontejos" in 1785 with a darling little Pug prominent in the lower right-hand corner of the painting. This painting, said to be the most beautiful of all featuring a Pug, can be seen at the national Gallery of Art in Washington, D.C. as part of the Andrew Mellon collection.

A painting of George III (1760-1820) contains the appearance of a Pug dog, obviously belonging to his wife, Charlotte, Princess of Mecklenburg-Strelitz, who had several Pugs. And in the early 1800's Reinagle rendered several paintings and drawings of the breed illustrating the close-cropped ears fashionable at the time. In 1845 J.C. Bell did a painting of two Pugs, and in Vero Shaw's book, published in 1879 there is a reproduction of C. Burton Barber's Pug painting of "Tip." In 1899 Arthur Wardell's painting of a Pug was reproduced in *Lee's Modern Dogs* book. A Pug appears in Buffon's *Histoire Naturelle*, a framed copy of which is owned by the author.

It was also during the late 1800's that Pugs were popular on the advertising cards of that era. In 1880 William Hopkins painted his Pug, and a seated Pug by H. Simon is hung at the American Kennel Club.

In modern times, during the early days of Pugs in this country, the late artist Lillian Tiffany, while devoted to all breeds did some marvelous renditions of Pugs.

Today, during the 1970's, Mary De Camp of Grand View, New York, has distinguished herself with excellent pen and ink drawings that have graced stationery and have appeared in several of the Pug publications. They are also featured in a booklet published by Mary and Margaret Cameron entitled *Pugs and Poems*.

One of Mary's favorites is the drawing of her Pug, the late Bill Sykes, who carried a tennis ball around in his mouth all his life. That is, until he lost all his teeth. The drawing is one of the many endearing attitudes assumed by Pugs that Mary De Camp has captured in her art work and several of which adorn her High Tone Pugs Kennel stationery.

Mary has also been commissioned over the years to do individual paintings of dogs by their proud owners. A few of these com-

This early 20th century painting owned by Dr. and Mrs. Edward Patterson was a piano company advertisement many years ago and was later a Christmas card design.

A bronze clock, circa 1800, featuring a moving tail and tongue, which are motivated by the seconds ticking away. Owned by Puppen-theatersammlung, Munchen. Photo courtesy of C.A. Veldhuis, the Netherlands.

Another charming painting immortalizing the Pug is this painting of a little girl and her dog.

missions came from Joan Perry, Michael Weissman and Jim Moran.

THE PUG IN LITERATURE

Perhaps the first time the word "Pug" was recorded was in Howell's Dictionary of 1660. A Tate play produced in 1665 entitled *Cuckold's Haven* included the word Pugg, and it must be remembered that this word applied to "anyone held dear." To be referred to as "my little Pugg," was an honor indeed. Some light verse written by a man named Gay in 1728 makes reference to a Pug dog as does the text of David Garrick's play entitled *Lethe Aesop in the Shades*. In 1786 an Italian writer referred to the Pug as "a transplanted Hollander, carried thither from China." Thomas

A velvet jewelry board featuring the collection of Helen Bortner. Some of the pieces are in solid gold; others are of marcasite and enamel and some are studded with rubies. These treasured, valuable pieces have been collected through the years during which Helen has been devoted to this breed.

Above: A painting of Queen Victoria of England and her extensive family, circa 1875. Note the Pug dog in the lower left hand corner of this royal family portrait. **Below:** Two more variations on the Pug, from the Rowann Collection.

Bewick in 1790 made mention of the breed; an 1878 Harper's Weekly publication printed a picture entitled *"Bothered"*, showing a small dog bothering a Pug. *Stonehenge on the Dog,* published in 1879 devoted space to the Pug as did *Dogs of the British Islands* published in 1867 also by Stonehenge, who was actually J.H. Walsh.

In later years the *Hutchinson Encyclopedia* gave much space to reporting on the breed, as did Edward Ash's *The Practical Dog Book,* published in 1930, Rawson Lee's *Modern Dogs,* and Brian-Vesey Fitzgerald's *The Book of the Dog.*

Books devoted entirely to the breed, or even in part devoted to the breed, are too numerous to mention, but a book list can be obtained by contacting the American Kennel Club.

However, we must mention here that one of the first books published on the Pug was in 1905 entitled, *Hints on the Management of Black Pugs,* by L.J. F. Pughe and printed by the Times Printing Works in Northgate, England. It has become a collector's item.

A famous Edwin Magargee oil painting of a mother Pug and her puppies, from the collection of James Moran.

A stuffed pillow from an old design, owned by author Joan Brearley. Another of these was part of the exhibition entitled *Pugs, People and the Peter Chaplin Collection* in 1976 at the Swem Library, William and Mary College, Williamsburg, Virginia.

A bronze Pug bitch made by Wekstatt Hubert Gerhard in 1600, owned by Staatiche Kunstsammlung Kassel. Courtesy C.A. Veldhuis, the Netherlands.

PUGS AND FAMOUS PEOPLE

Alyce M. Andre of Vienna, Virginia, has in her possession a book dated 1892 and entitled *Famous Pets of Famous People*, by Eleanor Lewis. It is dedicated to Maud Howe Elliott, a great animal lover in her day, and owner of a Pug named Sambo. A picture of them is included on the first page of the book.

Maud Howe's friend, Harriet Beecher Stowe, author of *Uncle Tom's Cabin*, published in 1852, was also a Pug fancier and had two Pugs named Punch and Missy. Punch was a gift to Mrs. Stowe after being selected from a breeder in Boston and presented to Mrs. Stowe in Hartford, Connecticut in 1881.

Each winter Punch would accompany Mrs. Stowe to Florida by train and also traveled with her abroad, where he spent much time on the crimson sofa in the Captain's quarters aboard the passenger ships on which Mrs. Stowe sailed. Punch frequently hid sugared almonds under the couch which he did not particularly care for but was too kind to reject from his admirers. He also hid under that same couch during rough weather! He enjoyed the privileges of the pilot house, but was known to stay close to the side of the ship when being walked during his constitutionals because of his fear of the sea.

In September 1883 Punch was stolen from Mrs. Stowe and although his disappearance was widely reported in the papers, and

An interesting Pug figurine from the collection of the Rowann Kennels.

A signed bronze by Doris Lindner of a crouching Pug, also owned by the Rowann Kennels.

An old Ironstone plate from England featuring a Pug dog with the early English type head. From the collection of James Moran.

A Pug charm denoting membership in the Byou des Mopsordens. The silver charm hangs from a blue ribbon. Photograph courtesy of C.A. Veldhuis.

Original punch needle hooked rug of three Victorian type Pug dogs, designed and worked by Dr. Robert L. Gossweiler of Timonium, Maryland. Dr. Gossweiler has, on occasion, donated a rug of this type as a trophy at parent club Specialty shows.

a reward was offered, he remained among the missing until March, 1885, when he was recognized and reclaimed at the New Haven dog show! His joy at returning home with Mrs. Stowe was heartwarming!

During his absence Mrs. Stowe had acquired "Missy" from the same gentleman who had given her Punch. Missy was an English import and it was difficult for Mrs. Stowe to cherish one more than the other. However, for those of us who have viewed the photograph of Punch and Missy it is clear to see that Punch earned his prize at the dog show. Missy's ears stood straight out from her head! Mrs. Stowe loved them equally and for all the rest of their days.

As the Pug came to prominence in this country more and more famous people came to know it and love it also. Just as it had become the fashion for theatrical people and glamorous movie stars to be accompanied by teams of Russian Wolfhounds as they were called in those days, there were those who came to know and love the spunky little Pug dogs that had for centuries charmed the royalty of Europe.

By the 1970's there was an impressive list of famous people who were advocates of the breed: Nobel Prize-winner Patrick White,

Senator Lowell Weicker of Connecticut, movie stars Joan Blondell, Eddie Albert, Sylvia Sidney, Lena Horne, Richard Burton, radio personality Tex McCrary, fashion designer Valentino (Garavani), Lee Radziwill, Cecil Beaton and Jan Miner, who is Madge the Manicurist on the Television commercials.

Comedienne Kay Thompson also promoted the breed by making a Pug the pet of Eloise, a little girl she created for a series of books, who lived her life at New York City's famous Plaza Hotel. Among modern day royalty the Vicomtesse de Ribes owned a Pug, and as mentioned elsewhere in this book, Prince Rainier of Monaco. However, where royalty today is concerned the title of chief advocates of the breed must be bestowed upon the Duke and Duchess of Windsor.

Their first Pugs, Disraeli, Trooper, and Davy Crockett endeared the breed to them forever, and in almost all photographs

A rare old figurine of a Pug dog from the extensive collection at the Rowann Kennels.

Another of Diana Mulhern's original needlepoint pillows. Diana also does ceramics featuring paintings of Pugs. This one in a series of head studies of the Pug is 20″ by 20″.

of the couple at home or while traveling they are accompanied by one or more of their Pugs. The royal couple was frequently seated at ringside during the parent specialty shows, and they were more than willing to present trophies at these events and can be complimented on all the attention they brought to our breed.

THE PETER CHAPIN SHOW

In 1976 Her Royal Highness, the Duchess of Windsor, was the Honorary Chairman of an exhibition of Pug books, figures, graphics and other memorabilia held at the J. Edward Zollinger Gallery in Swem Library, College of William and Mary in Williamsburg, Virginia. The exhibition featured the Pug collections of Mr. and Mrs. R.J. Dusek who submitted 88 pieces, and Mr. William D. Eppes' forty-five pieces. They were on view October 20th through December 1st. Artist Barbara Comfort also submitted an oil portrait of a Pug and three life-size pressed wood cut-outs of Pugs.

Both the exhibition and the catalogue were "Dedicated with Honor and Affection to the Memory of one of Pugdom's greatest

Life-size plaster Pug dog purchased in Chambersburg, Pennsylvania by Marianne Johnson of Medford, Ohio.

A terra cotta piece, circa 1880, with glass eyes, owned by Mrs. George J. Goodwin Jr. of St. Petersburg, Florida.

Author Joan Brearley has captured the likeness of one of her Pug puppies in a needlepoint pillow design. The attractive pillow is done in shades of green with a pale pink background.

fanciers: His Royal Highness The Duke of Windsor (1894-1972)". It is interesting to note, however, that the Chapin Library was established in 1937 by Mr. and Mrs. Howard Chapin in memory of—not their Pug, but—their black Cocker Spaniel named Peter Chapin!

Aside from the above-mentioned Pug exhibition the Peter Chapin Library includes over twenty-five hundred books, with at least one of every American Kennel Club recognized breed. The collection also includes "The Dumb Witness," a mystery story by Agatha Christie, in which, you guessed it, the "dumb witness" was a dog!

The library, incidentally, is also the archive for the official breed magazine, *Pug Talk*, published by the Pug Dog Club of America.

OTHER IMPORTANT PUG DOG COLLECTIONS

Most all Pug fanciers today have at least a few pieces of art or a

Two examples of the Pug's incorporation into advertising shortly after the turn of the century. One ad is for Prof. Horsford's Baking Powder and the other for the Bush, Bull and Roth Company which advertised itself as the "largest dry goods dealers" in Watertown, New York.

dusty book or two devoted to our beloved Pugs. But some are very fortunate to have come into the possession of truly fine, rare and treasured pieces or collections of great value. Among the largest and most valuable is that of James Cavallaro, who became heir to the collection of Richard Paisley after his tragic death in an automobile accident in 1973. Helen Bortner of Baltimore, Maryland, is another with a priceless collection of paintings, glass, bronze, ceramics, and other pieces occupy many walls and curio cabinets in her home.

We have all heard about the lovely collection belonging to James Trullinger, important pieces owned by Shirley and Rayne Thomas, Marianne Johnson of Medford, Ohio, Diana and Ken Mulhern of Santa Ana, California, James Moran, and the Rowan Kennels in Lincoln, Nebraska, to name a few. It is the ultimate wish of the author that at some time in the future a Dog Museum of great importance will be established where all these treasures may be shared by everyone in one place for all time!

Bonjor's Jane Addams, handled and owned by Bonna Webb of Middletown, Ohio, shown winning at the 1976 Livonia Kennel Club show under breeder-judge Gus Wolf. The sire was Ch. Eston's Abou Ben Addam ex Ch. Bonjor's Clara Barton.

Chapter 14
Pug Dog Clubs

It cannot be emphasized too strongly how important it is for Pug owners to belong to a Pug dog club. An all-breed club is also important, but a Specialty club will certainly give every owner full information about the breed and the fancy as well. Whether you intend to show your Pug or not, there is a lot of benefit to be derived from associating with other owners within the club atmosphere and activities that do not necessarily involve only show dogs.

The breeder of your dog can acquaint you with a local club in your area or you can contact the American Kennel Club at 51 Madison Avenue, New York, New York 10010, for the name of the parent club whose secretary can put you in contact with the regional club in your area.

PUG DOG CLUBS

We must all look to our specialty breed clubs for guidance and information if we are truly interested in our breed. The various clubs which oversee the good and welfare of Pugs are a wonderful way for newcomers to learn about the breed and about showing and obedience and to keep up with all the latest news.

Usually fanciers belong to one specialty club devoted exclusively to the Pug and then also one all-breed dog club. It is advisable to recommend membership in a club even for the pet Pug owner.

A list of the various breed clubs follows. Correspondence with the one nearest to your area will bring any information you might require in regard to membership.

PUG DOG CLUB OF AMERICA
David Miller, Corresponding Secretary
R.D. 1, Twin Lakes
Port Deposit, Maryland 21904

CITY OF ANGELS
PUG CLUB, INC.
Mary Phillips, Secretary
10078 McBroom Street
Sunland, Calif. 91040

Left: Kesander's Sassy Lassy going Best of Winners and Best of Opposite Sex for a three-point major on the way to championship. The judge at this 1976 Wisconsin Kennel Club Show was Mrs. James Carter. Owner handled by Bob Anderson, Naperville, IL. **Below:** Ch. Blaylock's Stormy Stranger, owned by Ken and Diana Mulhern.

Right: Ch. Dandy's Doryson Buccaneer, co-owned by Mrs. W.M. Braley and Mrs. R.D. Hutchison of Tampa, FL. **Below:** Ch. Blaylock's Bold Ruler, owned by Mrs. Rolla Blaylock.

Above: Am., Mex. Ch. McGee's Darklu of Sapphire winning Bet of Opposite Sex at the 1970 city of Angels Pug Club Specialty. Keith Brown judged, Gordon Phillips handled. **Left:** Ch. Friar Tuck winning at a 1968 show. Tuck was the first champion for Ron and Shari Higman of Miami, Florida.

International Champion Bill's Boy of Larimar, undefeated for his championship with 2 Toy Group wins, and the sire of 12 champions. Owner bred and handled throughout his show ring career by Hazel Martens, Larimar Ranch Kennels, San Diego, California.

Ch. Kesander's Double Debbel going Best of Breed at the 1976 Louisville Kennel Club under judge Nick Calicura. Handled by Lorraine Heichel for breeder-owners Jean and Bob Anderson of Naperville, IL.

GREAT LAKES PUG CLUB, INC.
Mrs. Mildred Winders, Secretary
P.O. Box 335
Rochelle, Illinois 61068

BLUEBONNET PUG DOG CLUB
Gwendolyn Bennet,
Corresponding Secretary
Route 1, Box 12
Tennessee Colony, Texas 75861

PUG DOG CLUB
OF MARYLAND, INC.
Marjorie D. May
Corresponding Secretary
10123—52nd Avenue
College Park, Maryland 20740

PUG DOG CLUB
OF GREATER CINCINNATI
Miss Helen Klopmeier, Secretary
8419 Burns Avenue
Cincinnati, Ohio 45216

PUG DOG CLUB OF GREATER
NEW YORK, INC.
Mrs. Shirley Thomas
Corresponding Secretary
43-64 Bowne Street
Flushing, New York 11355

GREATER MILWAUKEE
PUG CLUB, INC.
Barbara Nook, Secretary
8912 W. Rohr Avenue
Milwaukee, Wisonsin 53225

TAMPA BAY PUG CLUB, INC.
Betty Page, Corresponding Secretary
555 Robin Hood Drive
Merritt Island, Florida 32952

PUGET SOUND PUG DOG CLUB
Marilyn Brantley
Corresponding Secretary
P.O. Box 744
Oak Harbor, Washington 98277

Right: Shirrayne's Hot Shot, owned by Jeffrey and Mariette Keefe, Piccadilly Pugs, Worcester, MA. Photo by L. Allard. **Below:** Am., Can. Ch. Sheffield's Sunday Punch, bred and owned by Mrs. Paul L. Shriver of Baltimore.

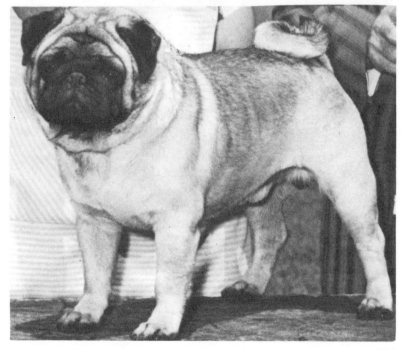

Ch. Pugtowne's Short Fuse pictured winning at the 1965 Long Island Kennel Club show. She produced 10 champions as a foundation for the Pugtowne Kennels Oceanside, New York. John J. Marsh, owner, handled.

Movin' on! Owned by Berna and Ernest Semrad of Enid, Oklahoma, this Pug has traveled all over the mid-west for nine years with the trailer crew. Whenever you travel with your Pug by car or van, ensure his safety by keeping him in a wire pen.

Australian Ch. Westcourt Ebony Kalif, bred by N. Downey and owned by Mr. and Mrs. G. Burgess and N. Downey of Victoria, Australia.

Above: Am., Can., Cuban Ch. Phyls Donna Annabelle, dam of the famous Int. Ch. Pugville's Mighty Jim, owned by Filomena Doherty, shown winning a Toy Group many years ago. **Below:** The old-timers! Ch. Ivanwold Portia's Pride, 13 years of age, and her 10 year old daughter, Ch. Ivanwold Morgan Le Fey, enjoy the sunshine at the home of Mrs. Edith Wright in Arlington, VA. Portia produced six champions, and there are few Ivanwold Pugs that do not descend from this great bitch. Their breeders were Dr. and Mrs. Edward Patterson of Destin, FL.

Right: Ch. Ah-Ya Gung Ho Murphy "at work" at the typewriter! Owner Mrs. R.D. Hutchison of Tampa. **Below:** Ianlee Beau Bengy, owner Mrs. S.E. Clements, Essex, England. Bengy qualified for the 1977 Crufts show and has done well at championship shows. He is the grandson of Am. Ch. Laughing Water Mi Wan of Hazelbridge.

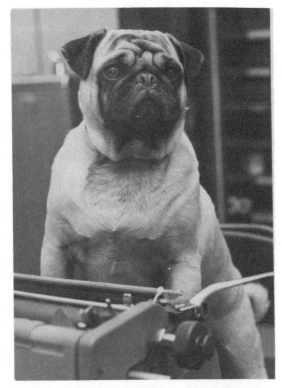

Ch. Angel's Ace Hi
of Carol Mar is pictured
here winning Best of
Breed at a 1976 show.

Sabbaday Favorite Son, pictured at nine months, owned by Polly J.
Lamarine, Silvertown Pugs, Meriden, Connecticut. The 1974 photo is
by Evelyn Shafer.

Ch. Fiesta Fahey wins Best of Breed at the 1964 Pug Dog Club of America Specialty under Edwin Pickhardt. Cleveland Amory presents the Walter C. Foster Memorial Trophy donated by the Duke and Duchess of Windsor. Fiesta is owned, bred and shown by Mrs. Lee Fahey, Kansas City, Missouri.

FOREIGN PUG CLUBS

THE PUG DOG CLUB
Mrs. D.M. Johnson
"The Old Parsonage Kennels"
Hoton, Nr Loughborough
Leicestershire, England

THE NORTHERN
PUG DOG CLUB
Mr. Frank Laver, Secretary,
Meadow House
Todwick
Sheffield, Yorkshire
531/OHG, England

THE SCOTTISH PUG DOG CLUB
Mrs. T. Greenhill-Reid, Secretary
Ardglass, Milton Road East
Edinburgh 15, Scotland

PUG DOG CLUB OF FINLAND
Miss Leila Gauffin, Secretary
Lemmikkitie 17
Hiekkaharju, Finland

THE PUG DOG CLUB
OF EAST AFRICA
Mr. I. Yorke-Davis, Hon. Secretary
P.O. Box 24832
Karen, Kenya, East Africa

THE IRISH PUG DOG CLUB
Mrs. Mary Whelan
Honorable Secretary
5 Blackrock Lodge
Blackrock, Co.
Dublin, Ireland

THE NORTHERN TRANSVAAL
PUG BREEDERS CLUB
Mrs. Delene Nicolau
341 Celliers Ave.
Lyttleton Manor Ext. 1
Verwoerdburg 0140
Transvaal, S.A.

"COMMEDIA," VEREENIGING
VAN FOKKERS EN LIEFHEBBERS
VAN DE
MOPSHOND IN NEDERLAND
Miss Christina A. Veldhuis
Bakenbergseweg 158
Arnhem, Nederland

THE PUG DOG CLUB OF AMERICA

The Pug Dog Club of America is considered the parent club for the breed. They have held a specialty show every year since their first was held on Feb. 10, 1957. Originally it was held around the February Westminster Kennel Club date, but since 1967 they have been held in the Fall.

A history of the club's early years states that the actual date of the formation of the club is unknown. However, American Kennel Club records reveal that there was a Pug Dog Club of America as early as 1931 and this group held their first specialty in conjunction with the Morris and Essex Kennel Club Show in Madison, New Jersey, in 1937.

Right: Ch. Broughcastl Brigadir of Doun, owned by Douglas Huffman of House Springs, Missouri, and bred by Mrs. Rolla Blaylock, shown winning at the 1970 Quincy Kennel Club show.
Below: Harloo Mellissa, bred by Harry and Lou Green, Harloo Kennels in Shropshire, England.

Left: Ch. Abbeville Personality, one of the great Pugs, photographed by famous dog photographer, Tauskey. **Below:** Can., Am. Ch. Cielo's Fleur de Lis going Winners Bitch at the 1967 Pug P.D.C.A. Specialty under Mrs. Rigden. Owner handled by Mrs. Shirley Limoges, Bernalee Pugs, Ontario, Canada.

Right: Ch. Higman's Bold N' Brassy. Owners Ron and Shari Higman, Miami. **Below:** Future Ch. Our Tiger Higgs with handler Pam Tackett.

Ch. Bleuridges Bobo of Tuffy pictured winning at a recent Spartan-
burg, South Carolina show. The sire was Ch. Prelly's Rolly Roister ex
Gore's Tammy. Owned by Bunny Osborn, Vero Beach, Florida.

Ch. Anidee's Dark Secret winning Best of Opposite sex from the open Black Class. Sire was Merriveen With Cream ex Am. and Mex. Ch. Mcgee's Darklu of Sapphire. Show by Gordon and Mary Phillips Anidee Pugs, Shadow Hills, California.

Left: Am., Can. Ch. Jolley Li'l Mo-Jo Sachjon, handled by Gene Hahnlen for owners Paul and Ruth Jolley, Seattle. **Below:** Ch. Pugtowne's Short Fuse, handled by John J. Marsh, and her son Ch. Pugtowne's Canadian Caper, handler Elaine Marsh.

Right: Ch. Ivanwold High Barbary, pictured winning the Breed under Joseph Rowe. Co-owned by John Cobb and Dr. Edward Patterson. **Below:** Ch. Bleuridges Link, handled by Barbara Braley who co-owns with E.G. Willard. Judge was Joseph Rowe at this 1974 event.

Left: Ch. Peter Boy of Larimar, owned and shown by Hazel Martens of San Diego. **Below:** Ch. Jackpots Wheeler Dealer pictured winning under judge Joan Alexander. Bred, owned and handled by Creighton Jackson, Jackpot Pugs, Spring, Texas.

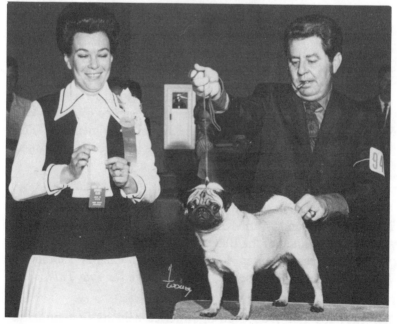

The club dissolved during the following years. But it was in 1950 when it is said the present day Pug Dog Club of America was started in a posh New York City hotel room. That first meeting brought together a dedicated group of Pug fanciers comprised of the most important people in the breed at that time, among them Mrs. Filomena Doherty and Dr. Nancy Riser of the Vikiri line; "Sis" Sewall, of Tarralong; Mr. and Mrs. Arthur Cassler of Melcroft; the late Fred Greenly and Mrs. Greenly, Mrs. Don Smith of North'boro, Miss Harriet Smith, and the late Walter Foster and Mrs. Foster of Fostoria fame. A financial statement places the date prior to 1950, since it read, "Cash on Hand, February 10, 1950, $286.33. It also listed dues from two people in 1949 and 9 people in 1950. Collected dues during the period of these early 1950's included names of Mr. and Mrs. John Marsh, J. Fred Jacobberger, Mrs. A.C. Gregoroff, the Arthur Casslers and the George Bartos, and Mrs. Sewall.

The first dated minutes were for a December 10, 1954 meeting at the Penn-Sherwood Hotel in Philadelphia with eleven members and two guests in attendance. Seventeen new members were voted into the club at this meeting including James Trullinger who even today, serves the breed as a judge and author of a book on the breed. It is believed that Walter Foster served as the club's first president. Future meetings, it was decided, would be held the day before the Westminster Kennel Club show in New York City to insure the widest possible attendance.

The Pug Dog Club of America continued to grow as the years passed. By 1961 the club had an insignia designed by artist Mrs. Marjorie Van Vloten, and decals were available for members. This was the year the club got busy working on a handbook for prospective members.

PUG TALK

The parent club magazine was started in 1966. It was called *Pug Talk*, and Jack and Mimi Keller were the original editors. Jack was also the founder of the Bluebonnet Pug Club in Texas. Unfortunately, he passed on in 1970. The Peter Chapin Library in Williamsburg, Virginia, serves as the archive for *Pug Talk*.

THE FIRST FUTURITY

In 1967 the Pug Dog Club of America held its first futurity.

Above: Ch. Baronrath Travilah, owned by Mary B. Hecht, is pictured winning under judge Joan Alexander at the 1969 Old Dominion Kennel Club Show. **Left:** John Pomara's Shirrayne's Elegant Echo pictured winning at the 1974 El City Kennel Club show. Handled by breeder Shirley Thomas for the owner.

Ch. Little Bear, owned by Norman G. Pittinger of Garrison, Maryland, cools off with a cold towel while waiting to go into the show ring.

Above: Ch. Blaylock's County Judge, multiple Group and Specialty winner, is pictured winning the 1965 Great Lakes Pug Club Specialty show under the well-known breeder of yesteryear, Mrs. Edna Hillgamyer. Presenting the trophy is Gordon Winders. Owner, Mrs. Rolla Blaylock. **Opp., top:** Winner of the Grand Sweepstakes at the 1974 Pug Dog Club of America Specialty show was 11 month-old Harper's Priscilla Lorene, handled by Alan L. Harper. The trophy presenter is the distinguished Pug breeder, Mrs. Suzanne Rowe. Owned by Harper's Pugs, Jacksonville, Florida. **Opp., bottom:** Perseus of Paramin, bred by Mrs. Margo Raisin of the Paramin Pugs, Yorkshire England and sold to Mr. and Mrs. Stevenson of Tasmania, Australia. The sire was Ch. Adoram Damon Dillypin ex Primrose of Paramin.

Over the years, a great many celebrities have come to own Pugs, and
to appreciate them as fine pets and show dogs. Here, in a photo
taken more than 20 years ago, singing star Lena Horne, who has owned and bred Pugs presents a trophy to handler Jack Funk for Champion Blaylock's Mar-Ma-Duke. Mar-Ma-Duke's owner was Gordon
Winders, of Skokie, Illinois. This particular occasion was the 1959
Pug Dog Club of America Specialty show, which was held that year at
the Hotel McAlpin, in New York City. Judging at the event, and also
pictured here is James W. Trullinger.   **Opp.:** Goodwin's Putt Putt,
bred/owned/ handled by Mrs. G. J. Goodwin, St. Petersburg.

A magnificent head study of Filomena Doherty's American, Canadian, Cuban and Bermudian Champion Pugville's Mighty Jim. Photograph is by the famous dog photographer, Tauskey.

Harry Smith was the futurity chairman and the event was recorded as a huge success. James Trullinger was the judge, and from the twenty-five entries chose Smith's Tar Baby of Gore as the winner with his sister, Gore's Gabrielle, as Best of Opposite Sex. Both were bred by Mr. and Mrs. Herman Gore of Kentucky.

In 1967 the club was voted to include annual awards for Sire, Dam and Breeder of the Year categories.

THE CLUB HANDBOOK

The Club's *Handbook* was available in time for the Specialty show in 1967, and by 1970 it was voted that a brochure be prepared to be mailed by the secretary to those inquiring about Pugs. The brochure pointed out the advantages of owning Pugs, the breed Standard, and a history of the breed.

In 1972 the age limit for membership was dropped and in 1973 the Pug Dog Club of America was incorporated.

PUG DOG CLUB OF AMERICA SPECIALTY WINNERS

Feb. 10, 1957	Ch. Tarralong Phillip, S.V. Bellinger
Feb. 9, 1958	Ch. Blaylocks Mar Ma Duke, G. Winders
Feb. 8, 1959	Ch. Blaylocks Mar Ma Duke, G. Winders
Feb. 7, 1960	Ch. Blaylocks Mar Ma Duke, G. Winders
Feb. 12, 1961	Ch. Star Jade of Northboro, Sabbaday Kennels
Feb. 11, 1962	Ch. Sabbaday Echo, Sabbaday Kennels
Feb. 10, 1963	Ch. Sabbaday Echo, Sabbaday Kennels
Feb. 9, 1964	Ch. Fiesta Fahey, Mrs. L. Fahey
Feb. 14, 1965	Ch. Fiddler Fahey, Mrs. L. Fahey
Feb. 13, 1966	Ch. Bassetts Dapper Dan of Gore, Mr. & Mrs. Bassett
Sept. 10, 1967	Ch. Satina, R. Paisley
Oct. 11, 1968	Ch. Crowells Little Joe of Gore, A. Crowell
Oct. 10, 1969	Ch. Belcrest Jim Dandy, Belcrest Kennels
Sept. 11, 1970	Ch. Heritage Tom Cat of Gore, B.A. Minella
Sept. 17, 1971	Ch. Baronrath Baron of Kokusai, M.F. & Y. Davis
Sept. 15, 1972	Ch. Carbon Copy of Ju Lims, J.C. Fischer
Sept. 14, 1973	Ch. Belcrest Aristocratic, Belcrest Kennels
Sept. 13, 1974	Ch. Bleuridges Link, B. Craley & E.G. Willard
Sept. 12, 1975	Ch. Bonjors Tuff Jorgell Do It, B. Webb & D. Huffman
Sept. 11, 1976	Ch. Sabbaday Kidds Capricorn, S. Sidney

About the Author

Joan Brearley is the first to admit that animals in general—and dogs in particular—are a most important part of her life. Since childhood there has been a steady stream of dogs, cats, birds, fish, rabbits, snakes, alligators, etc., for her own personal menagerie. Over the years she has owned over 30 breeds of pure-bred dogs, as well as countless mixtures, since the door was never closed to a needy or homeless animal.

A graduate of the American Academy of Dramatic Arts where she studied acting and directing, Joan started her career as an actress, dancer, and writer for movie magazines. She studied ballet at the Agnes DeMille Studios in Carnegie Hall and was with an oriental dance company which performed at the Carnegie Recital Hall. She studied journalism at Columbia University and has written for radio, television and magazines, and was a copywriter for some of the major New York City advertising agencies.

While a television producer-director for a major network she worked on "Nick Carter, Master Detective;" "Did Justice Triumph;" and news and special feature programs. Joan has written, cast, directed, produced and, on occasion, starred in television film commercials. Joan was included in the *Directory of the Foremost Women In Communications* in 1969, and the book, *Two Thousand Women of Achievement* in 1971. She is also a member of the Screen Actors Guild.

Her accomplishments in the dog fancy include breeding and exhibiting top show dogs, writer, lecturer and columnist on various magazines and author of over twenty books on dogs and cats, including *This Is the Irish Setter, This Is the Siberian Husky, The Book of the Doberman Pinscher,* etc. For five years she was Executive Vice-President of the Popular Dogs Publishing Company and editor of *Popular Dogs* magazine, the national prestige publication for the fancy at that time. Her editorials on the status and welfare of animals have been reproduced as educational pamphlets by dog clubs and organizations in many countries of the world.

Joan is just as active in the cat fancy, and in almost as many

Joan Brearley with her Pug, Shirrayne's Hong Kong Jade East.

capacities. The same year her Afghan Hound, Ch. Sahadi Shikari, won the Ken-L Ration Award as Top Hound of the Year, one of her Siamese cats won a comparable honor in the cat fancy. She has owned and/or bred almost all breeds of cats. Many of her cats and dogs are Best In Show winners and have appeared in magazines and on television. For several years she was editor of the Cat Fanciers Association Annual Yearbook, and her book, *All About Himalayan Cats*, was published in 1976.

Joan looks forward to the near future when she will once again breed dogs at her Sahadi Kennels and Cattery to continue her line of dogs which excel in the breed rings, obedience trials, in the field and on the race tracks.

316

Index